To John
Enjoy your cat
And your warmth.

Gary [signature]

The Feline Mystique

A Man's Guide to Living With Cats (and/or Women)

by

Gary Lukatch

Bloomington, IN authorHOUSE® Milton Keynes, UK

AuthorHouse™
1663 Liberty Drive, Suite 200
Bloomington, IN 47403
www.authorhouse.com
Phone: 1-800-839-8640

AuthorHouse™ UK Ltd.
500 Avebury Boulevard
Central Milton Keynes, MK9 2BE
www.authorhouse.co.uk
Phone: 08001974150

© 2007 Gary Lukatch. All rights reserved.

No part of this book may be reproduced, stored in a retrieval system, or transmitted by any means without the written permission of the author.

First published by AuthorHouse 1/17/2007

ISBN: 978-1-4259-8924-8 (sc)

Printed in the United States of America
Bloomington, Indiana

This book is printed on acid-free paper.

For Jacquie

Acknowledgments

As usual, nobody helped me with the writing of this book. No one read the manuscript, no one suggested additions or deletions, no one proofread anything, no one offered to be my agent or publisher, no one edited anything. I did it all on my own. I would have liked some help, and there are those critical and jealous souls who probably think I should have had help, but, too bad, no help. There was, of course, some research involved. So, looking back, I guess I should acknowledge all the cats I have ever known and: tolerated, loved, hated *(especially the one that sprayed my $300 Coogle sweater),* sheltered, fed, stroked, invited into my house, run over *(okay, I really didn't, it just sounded amusing to put it in here),* adopted in a mutually beneficial relationship of understanding and comfort, and was adopted by.

Also, quite naturally, thanks go to all the women I have known in my life. Again, with varying degrees of: affection, dislike, wonder, pleasure, hatred, enjoyment, awe, magnanimity, comfort, uncertainty, amazement and lust. You all (mostly) added immeasurably to my life and it has been an experience knowing each of you. With just one exception, I'd do you all over again.

Gary Lukatch
Summer 2006

Introduction

So, Men! College is finally behind you. You're out in the world, making a living, enjoying your job and your profession. You've bought your first upscale car, you're about to think about upgrading your living space from an apartment to a nice condo or even a small house. You're making good money and living the good life. Your social life is coming along nicely and the women you meet and date are fun and interesting and great playmates. No strings attached, at least for the moment.

But, even as you enjoy your life and all the good things in it, you gradually realize something may be missing. A companion. A partner. A possible soul-mate with whom to share your new-found prosperity and lifestyle. In short, a female roommate. A girl friend to share your living space as well as your life. You are beginning to think about something more serious than just a weekend sleepover. No, you haven't yet met the right girl with whom to share your home, but you're thinking about her and wondering when you'll meet her. And you're also wondering what it will be like to share your space with a woman, hopefully with a woman you love, but just possibly with a woman you like a lot, and whom, you also suspect, you will never marry.

It's a scary thing and a big step to take. I know, I know, your first thought is: SEX - anytime, anywhere, anywhen. Which, of course, is all we men really want anyway. Naturally however, guys, along with all that great nonstop sex, you also have to ----- LIVE WITH A WOMAN! Hmmmm. Yep, you'll have pretty much unlimited access to all that great sex you've just been getting on a sometimes basis. But, see, Guys, the funny thing about that initial sexual attraction is it just doesn't keep the same degree of heat for a long period of time. The hotter the fire, the shorter the burn. Your relationship with your female roommate changes, and becomes more like partnership. Or companionship. Oh, the sex is still there and still great - well, good, anyway - but in a subtly different way. And other things become more important - at least to her! Like companionship. And partnership. And mutual caring.

Keep in mind, Men, such an undertaking is not something to be entered into lightly, as any male who has ever known a female from the age of three up can testify. Women are tough roommates - or girlfriends - or wives - or whatever. And, let's face it, Guys, as much as we dearly love women, they aren't men and they can be difficult and demanding and hard to get along with. They look at the world differently from us, which can be fun and exciting, but can also be frustrating and annoying and hard to put up with.

So, what to do? Is there any way a man can prepare himself for living with a woman? Is there anything a man can do to get ready for what will probably turn out to be the biggest change in his life? Well, Guys, yes, as a matter of fact, there is. You **can** have a pre-female relationship that will prepare you for living with your woman of choice. Before you enter into a live-in relationship with a woman, before you take **The Big Step**, you have the chance to practice what it will most probably be like.

And that, after this long-winded introduction, is what this book is all about. Living with a Cat.

What, you say? A cat? What the hell do cats have to do with women? Ah, Guys, if you only knew *(which, one hopes, you will, because that's the whole purpose of this book!)*. If you can live successfully with a cat

- and, more importantly, if the cat can live successfully with you! - having a woman in the house will be a piece of cake.

So, guys, OK. Living with a cat can be a good thing, mainly because it will give you practice for **The Real Thing**. I'll say it again -- if you can live with a cat you can live with a woman! Yes, amazing as it may seem, cats and women are made of the same stuff. If a man can live with *(he'll never be able to completely understand)* cats, he can at least make a start to figuring out how to live with a woman *(see previous italics!)*.

As most men already know, guys are usually dog people. Dogs are our best friends, pets and slaves. Dogs are eager to please and they let us know it. Dogs crave our affection and will do anything to get it. Men love their dogs, because dogs love them. Unreservedly, without complaint, without hassles, unconditionally, completely and without reservations. Which, aside from sex (with a woman, naturally), is what most men really want. Love without questions, problems, demands. Stepford dogs.

Cats, on the other hand, are aloof, disdainful, patronizing, haughty, arrogant, lordly, proud, snobbish and supercilious. They allow us to inhabit their world *(as they see it)*, to give them food and to furnish them with a comfortable living space. Remind you of anyone you know, Guys?

Cats take great pains to let us poor men know they don't really need us; rather, they put up with us because we give them what they want - creature comforts. They allow us to give them all sorts of tasty cat foods and treats - food which is often better than we get ourselves. They allow us to give them a well-furnished cave-equivalent in which to relax and to feel they are the Lord of the Manor. They disdain the carpet-padded cat climbing tree for a $2,000 sofa on which to sharpen their claws. They allow us to inhabit their space, more as a tolerated being than as a fellow traveler. They allow us to play with them when they are just kittens and teenage cats, but when they become adult cats, they are too good for our petty needs and desires. Pet an adult cat when it doesn't want to be petted? Heaven forbid! *(Still doesn't sound familiar, Men?)*

They allow us to stroke them once in awhile *(when they're in the mood - not when we're in the mood)*. They allow us to open a can of tuna fish for them *(which they then greedily devour, confident in their superiority that their poorly-disguised greed will not be obvious to us, poor mortal human men that we are)*.

The dog eagerly rolls over onto its back, offering its stomach for the exquisite touch of a male human hand scratching it. The cat rubs up against us, which we think is a sign of its affection; the cat knows it is just leaving its scent on us so it will recognize us the next time it wants to prevail upon us to open a can of tuna fish for it.

Of course, cats do deign to give us little tokens of their affection, tokens which are usually more important to them than to us. A dog will bring back a thrown stick or frisbee for hours. A cat will bring us a dead mouse or lizard whenever she feels like it. Of course, the cat will only deliver this gift at the most inopportune moments, such as when we have our boss or a woman over for dinner and are trying desperately to impress them.

So, the cat shows us its affection by, in essence, belittling us, secure in its knowledge that we will accept its gift and never, ever complain about it or refuse it. It is, after all, a gift from The Cat - the all-important, center-of-its-own-universe CAT.

The immortal CAT. Scornful, disparaging, disdainful, proud, contemptuous, belittling, secure, needful but never letting let us know it. Now I ask you, men everywhere -- doesn't that really sound like a woman?

1. Cats

Choosing a Cat

Looking for a pet to share your living space? Not sure how to pick the best one? With dogs, it's easy. All a man needs to do is to be around a litter of fairly young pups and decide which one is the friendliest, cuddliest, cutest, happiest, most active, etc. Dogs let us know immediately which one we should choose. They cuddle up to us. They lick our face. They pee on us with happiness.

With cats, it's a little tougher. The best way is to find a kitten rather than a grown cat. Kittens are easier to pick, and, in most instances, they will pick us. Even at the tender kitten stage, they know enough to select the perfect human being to complement their kittenness. They'll let us know when they want us. They'll climb on us, extend their little kitten claws and try to get up near our face and neck, to let us know how cuddly and furry they are and how much better they would be to take home than a mere dog that will just fawn all over us. So we stroke them and marvel at how soft their fur is and we think how cute and friendly they are -- until we get them home and realize they've managed to rip a number of cute little irreparable kitten holes in our $300 cashmere sweater.

When checking the pet store for a cat, be especially careful of that cute little kitten in the corner, the one that wants you to think she's ignoring you and just waiting for someone better to come along and take her home. This is a kitten specialty, bred into young kittens from birth and nurtured strongly and for as long as possible by Mama Cat. When the kitten is old enough to be displayed in the pet store window, she is old enough to know the tricks of the adoption trade. The Cat knows it has several options at his disposal:

Trick 1: Look for an old woman who doesn't get out much. Pick one who is wearing nice clothes; she'll have enough money to feed you gourmet cat food. Plus she'll probably sleep with her windows open and you can take off at night for a little cat adventure. She'll have older, probably worn, furniture which she won't care if you ravage with your claws. She'll treat you like a little Princess, buying you catnip and having her long-suffering son-in-law put up a really nice cat tree for you to climb and rest in and survey the rest of your new domain.

Trick 2: Look for a young girl who wants a furry playmate to share her pink-spreaded, canopied bed. Girls around the age of nine or ten are the best. Not yet teenagers who will be too busy with boys to spend much time with you, but older than pre-schoolers who don't know how to treat a cat yet and will pull your ears and rub your fur the wrong way. Girls in this age group still need a confidante and will talk to you and fawn over you and force Daddy to buy you gourmet cat food and expect you to sleep with them on their really soft white bedspread that you can get dark cat hair all over with impunity. Of course, they will, from time to time, and especially on rainy days, dress you up in some cute little doll clothes and pretend you are a real person, trying to get you to drink a cup of non-existent tea and feeding you little tea biscuits. A small price to pay for all the other benefits.

Trick 3: Look for a dog-lover whose girlfriend dragged him to the pet store. When the girlfriend picks you up *(cute little kitten that you are),* and her dog-loving boyfriend condescendingly reaches over to pet you, you can meow pitifully and reach out your little kitten claws and snag the boyfriend's $300 cashmere sweater. *"So much for you, Buddy Roe! Your girlfriend's taking **me***

home and if you try to stop her you'll find out just what a dose of cat urine can do to the rest of your designer outfit. Meow, meow, meow, Sucker!"

Trick 4: Look for a young man who needs practice in living with a woman. These types should be easy to spot. They wander the pet store aisles in a sort of daze, not sure what they want, gazing wistfully at the puppies and parrots and easy-to-care-for goldfish. But he's read this book, and believed what he read, so he's on the lookout for just the right sort of kitten that will teach him what he needs to know about the art *(and it can be nothing less!)* of living with a cat - and, by extension, a woman. Mama Cat has trained her kittens well, and has ensured that they will always be able to spot this potential roommate easily: clean, but unkempt, hair; smooth shaven; khaki Dockers; loafers with no socks; cashmere sweater, easily snagged after he gets you home. And, of course, he's already bought a copy of *"Care and Feeding of Your Cat,"* and is carrying it in his Armani backpack. *(Even kittens have great eyesight and can see things like that).*

And so, Guys, you finally stop wandering those aisles and decide to linger in front of the kitten cage and you think, "Hey, they're just so damn cuddly, little balls of fur and claws. How could you not love them? Aren't they better than those slobbery, messy, all-over-you dogs? Won't they be so much less trouble and demanding than a dog?"

So they let us think!! Actually, a cat is more trouble, more difficult, more annoying, more hassle, more time-involved than any dog we will ever know. We own dogs; cats own us. Still don't recognize the Little Woman, Gentlemen?

2. Women

Choosing a Woman

Don't be fooled by the title of this Chapter, Boys. Don't ever delude yourselves into thinking we choose our women. The choice is theirs! They let us chase them until they catch us. We want women because we are genetically programmed to want them. We have to want them. Women, on other hand, only need us for reproductive reasons. And to supply them with shelter and food. And, of course, to bring them pretty baubles, after which they will allow us to have sex with them. Which is really all we want anyway. And which all women know. What would the world be without men? Lots of fat, happy women! Why are men always so nervous when proposing marriage? Because there is always the chance we'll get turned down - because women have the choice!

Oh, we parade up and down in front of them, preening our feathers and ruffling our fur, but it's they who have the choice - all we can do is parade and ruffle and preen. And hope they will choose us. They look us over like the craftiest of ancient caravan traders, checking for loose teeth and the ability to provide and the ability to protect and the ability to furnish a nice cave and bring them pretty baubles and protect their children.

Of course, Men, we also have some say in the matter of choice. And we can be just as crafty and selective as any woman. Can't we, Guys?! Damn Right! So settle in and pay attention to some selection criteria most men know in their mind, but have difficulty verbalizing. These are for you, Guys. Here are some criteria for you to consider when scanning the female horizon for your woman of choice.

1. Characteristics: Every man, of course, has his own criteria which he applies to a woman to see if she appeals to him. We're all different in our wants and needs, but some general criteria can still be stated here. Well-groomed (*but not fussy, and no hair sprayed into an immovable helmet*). Non-smear lipstick. Eye-shadow that enhances, but never makes her look like Dracula's Daughter. All appropriate appurtenances - arms, legs, ears, nose, eyes and brows, fingers and toes, etc; no more and no less. An extra nipple is just as bad as having only four toes on one foot. Perfectly-formed breasts (preferably two of them).

The ability to drive a car and to feel comfortable doing so. Having money in her hand and ready to hand over when standing in any line and waiting to pay for anything *(Most women stand patiently in line and, when finally asked to pay for their purchase, suddenly, snap out of their daze, open their purse, take out their wallet, and fumble through it looking for bills and the exact change in coins, thus effectively adding another five or ten minutes to the waiting time of every other person in line. Talk about an annoying habit! More on this later).*

Good with house plants. Can cook a turkey with one hand and pour your vodka and tonic with the other. Likes to watch football games on TV with you. Good at budgeting household expenses and paying bills on time. Sexually insatiable whenever you want her to be, and quiescent when you're watching football on TV. *(She must be able to switch on these last two characteristics instantaneously upon your demand).*

2. The Mother! *(Ominous organ music plays in the background)* If you want to see what your woman will look like in all-too-few years, try and get a peek at her Mother as early in the relationship as possible. And that, Guys, is probably what you have to look forward to in the years to come. So choose wisely and well. Is your woman a tall, willowy blonde with a perfect body? Is her Mother a short, stooped, fat, bald old woman? Be warned, Men. It's the shape of things to come.

3. Potential for Change. To put it as bluntly as possible - *We don't want change!*. Men hate change. We want, for ever and ever, the exact same woman we met and courted and fell for and asked to move in with us. We don't want a new hairstyle or clothes or a career or makeup. We were attracted to the woman we saw and she is who we want. Now and forever, world without end, amen. Not thinner or fatter or stronger or shorter or grayer or balder. No changes.

Don't believe me, Women? The proof that men hate change is easily presented.

Proof 1: The hairstyle. Men will find a hairstyle they like and will keep it for years. Sometimes decades. Women know this is true, as they often comment on it to their favorite man: "Honey, why don't you try a new hairstyle? It'll make you feel like a whole different person. And that crewcut! Honestly! That went out with pegged chinos and laker pipes." Ladies, we don't change our hairstyles because we don't want to change our hairstyles. We found the one we like and we're sticking with it. Just like the woman we found - we don't want her to change. Ever.

Proof 2: The Favorite Item of Clothing (shirt, baseball cap, etc). Men find a comfortable shirt, cap, whatever, that fits like it's supposed to and they wear it at every opportunity - around the house, watching TV, to the lake, etc. These favorite items of clothing drive women to distraction, and they try to throw them out at every opportunity. But we men always notice that suspicious bulge in the trash bag and we are able to rescue our shirt, cap, etc, from oblivion. We can not live without our security blanket.

So, Guys, your woman must be made aware of this male foible against change, and must be cautioned to live with it and deal with it. If she wants to play with makeup that makes her look different, let her do it with her friends and not with you. *(Unless, of course, it makes her look like Catherine Zeta-Jones or a porn star - then it's okay for a weekend).* Do not let her try out new hairstyles on you; let her know you don't like them. Right from the start, make sure she knows you will automatically dislike anything different about her, and work from there.

This will be an uphill battle all the way, Men, and it never ends throughout your time with your woman of choice. Why? C'mon, Guys, you should know this by now. Do I have to explain everything to you? OK, OK, pay attention out there. You will have to fight this fight forever, because all women love change. They like to change their hair color and style at least three times every year. They like to re-arrange the furniture in your home every six months or so. They like to change their clothes constantly. It is a well-known fact that every woman in the world would change her clothes a minimum of six times every day if she could afford to do so. They want a new car every few years. And shoes! Jeez, Guys, do I really need to tell you abut how many pairs of shoes a woman has to have to feel comfortable with her life? Check her closet before you get too seriously involved.

But worst of all, and the most difficult change to fight against, the inescapable, unalterable fact of life with a woman, is the basic fact that she wants to change YOU! Yep, a woman is just never happy with things the way they are, or the way she finds them. Nothing is ever good enough for her. This is yet another genetic predisposition in women, the Change Gene, that they have and we don't. Here's the rule, Guys. Write it large upon the slate of your future relationship with all women: Women love change for its own sake. They just can't leave well enough alone. A Satisfied Woman is an oxymoron.

Now, maybe this tendency to want to change things is okay in some areas. A new method of preparing your favorite meal, a new dress once a year to make her look more attractive to you, even a new car when the old one starts to make strange noises due to her having not checked the oil in three years. We can buy into those things, because they make our woman happy. But when they start in on us! Well, Katie bar the door! They pick and wheedle and maneuver and whine and cajole and threaten and chip, chip, chip away at us, knowing we'll give in the end, because these things usually don't matter as much to us as to the woman. The Chinese Water Torture has nothing on a persistent woman when it comes to getting what she wants. Of course, the more we give in to her incessant chipping, the more we give up and give away, until we are no longer the person we were, but are now the proud possession of the woman who has changed us into whatever she thinks she wanted.

The irony of such a situation, Guys, is, of course, that when the woman achieves what she started out to achieve, and changes us into what she thinks she wanted, she finds that she no longer wants the finished product. She has changed us into her ideal, her dream, her perfect mate, and now she finds that the end result is not so great after all. So she goes looking for someone else to change.

Get it? Women love and need change for its own sake! It's not the destination, it's the journey. Women are just never satisfied with what they have. They always want something different, something else, something newer, something better. This is woman's lot in life, and it is something which all men must understand and be able to deal with. If you change too much, in accordance with her constant chipping, you'll lose her because she won't want you anymore. If you resist too strongly, and remain more or less the same person you were when you got involved, you'll lose her because she can't change you at all.

So, what do we do? Strive for the middle ground, Men. Change just enough to satisfy her, but never so much that you become someone else. This won't be easy, and it requires years and years of knowing how to compromise and how to adjust to each and every new situation and potential change your woman wants to make. But you can do it! We are, after all, bigger and stronger than the woman. And now that we understand what she wants, and how insidious her chipping can be and what the results will inevitably be, we can resist and circumvent and bob and weave around her until she gives up *(temporarily, Men, only temporarily;*

remember that; she'll retreat grudgingly and regroup, only to return to the fray another day) and we can then relax in our favorite chair (still unmoved from where it has always been) and watch some football and drink some beer. And wait patiently for our woman to employ her primary weapon in the never-ending battle to get us to do what she wants us to do: sex. Which, of course, is all we really want anyway.

However, Men, through it all, always keep in mind the fact that when all is said and done, we're still the ones being chosen and not the ones doing the choosing. Face it, Guys, they've got us by the cojones, which, of course, is just where they want us. Genetically programmed to need them. We only THINK we've chosen them. Why is it so difficult to ask a woman to marry us? Because we know - we KNOW - that the choice is really theirs. And we're petrified they won't choose us!

Choice, guys, it's all about choice. And we don't get to choose. Unless, of course, we have lots and lots of money.

3. Cats

Bringing the cat home

The first thing a cat does in new surroundings is to explore them - every nook and cranny and unopened door and closet and cupboard and garage beam. The cat MUST know his new home as intimately as he does the back of his own paw. The cat will spend days - weeks - exploring his new home until he knows it all: where the best chair for curling up after a long night's prowling is; which cupboard door can be easily squeezed through to allow the cat access to food; which of your favorite houseplants has the best dirt for a little nighttime deposit of cat scat; where the box of Christmas tree ornaments is stored on top of the garage beams to offer a great hiding place when you come looking for the cat after she's clawed your new drapes into strips.

And, of course, where the cat food and cat food bowl are kept and when the cat can expect to be fed and with what. Guys, an initial word of advice: get your cat used to Plain Jane cat food **right away**! Otherwise, your cat will expect - nay, demand - gourmet cat food every day of its life. More on this tender subject later.

Spray those places you don't want the cat to sleep or use as a toilet with anti-cat spray, and re-treat those places at least weekly. Otherwise, the cat will take it upon itself to do whatever it damn well pleases in your (its!) home (cave). This new place is the cat's sanctum sanctorum, its hideaway from the rest of the world, its secret place, its cave. It must feel secure in its new home, and to do so means she will have to know the exact location of every item of furniture, every throw rug, every lamp, every towel, every cat toy.

The cat appropriates your home for itself as soon as you introduce it to its surroundings. The cat senses it will be living there, so it also knows, via its little internal cat antennae, that it must be able to find all of the important places in its new domicile as quickly and efficiently as possible. Places to hide. Places to play. Places to pee. Places to look down on you. Places to kill mice and birds it captures. The cat will soon adjust to its surroundings and will then proclaim its mastery of its new home and its pleasure with the home it has chosen by spraying your favorite cashmere sweater (*the one you bought after the kitten ripped its predecessor to shreds).* The cat is home.

*(**Ed. Note:** A quick and rather clever word on how to entice the cat into accepting its new home: when you bring the cat or kitten into your abode for the first time, before you put it down or let it roam free, put some butter on its paws. The cat will be intent on licking the butter off its paws for awhile, but its always-sharp senses will be hard at work evaluating and, well, sensing, that this new place may just be OK and is probably actually better than the place from whence it came. Plus, it's a hell of a lot better than being in a moving automobile! So, when the butter is gone, the cat will have given its new home tentative approval. How about that, sports fans?)*

4. Women
Exploring the Cave

The first thing a woman will do when entering her new potential home is to explore it. Open cupboards, closets, medicine cabinets, etc. She will peer into every nook and cranny to be certain she knows her new home (cave) as well as it is possible to know one's living space. When it comes to placing the new furniture *(or arranging - or re-arranging - the present furniture),* she will demand everything be placed exactly where she wants it, so she can find her way around even in the dead of night. A man's home may be his castle, but a woman's home is her sanctum sanctorum, her safe place, her protection from marauders, her cave.

A man's home is his hideaway from the world; a woman's home is her showplace for the world. A woman will push and shove and arrange and re-arrange and move and change everything in her new home until it suits her **just so!** *(Sorry, guys, actually she'll have **you** shoving and moving the furniture all around - my mistake).* A woman may be the biggest personal slob in town, but her domicile must be as perfect as her internal specifications can make it. It must be comfortable. It must be functional. It must ----- fit her!

And not only the inside of the cave, but also the outside -- approach routes (driveways), shrubbery, gardens, yards, bushes, trees, grass, flowers, decking -- everything! Everything and anything that proclaims to the world, "This is my domain! I, the Woman, declare it so! The Man I have chosen to provide for me and to protect me has enabled me to show the world that my domicile *(not 'his domicile,' of course!)* is the best cave in the neighborhood, and it will always remain the best and biggest and most luxurious. Or I won't give him any sex, which, of course, is all he really wants."

*(**Ed. Note:** A quick and rather clever word on how to entice a woman into accepting her new home: Naturally, when you bring your new woman into your home you can't spread butter on her hands and feet and wait for her to lick it off and give her new home tentative approval. Unless, of course, you have a really kinky woman, one who loved* Last Tango in Paris, *in which case, anything goes and you can spread butter*

wherever you want and the devil take the hindmost - so to speak!.

(But, guys, you can introduce a butter substitute. [No, Beanhead, not margarine! Think!] That's right, flowers. Or newly-baked bread. Or your ratty old furniture which has to be consigned to the garage. Or curtains that don't match, which will give her something to think about while her keen senses are busy evaluating and, well, sensing, the new abode and assuring her that it's not completely unsalvageable. By the time she's finished wandering around she will have given her new home her tentative approval. And at least it's better than being in a moving car!)

5. Cats

Food

Cats love gourmet cat food, real chicken livers *(even real chickens, if you can get them)*, cat goodies, live birds, milk, cheese, any kind of fish, and any kind of fowl. When you bring the cat to its new home, be especially careful when you give the cat its first meals. You **must** condition the cat to a lesser brand of cat food. If you give the cat Gourmet Goodies its first week in your *(its)* home, you are lost forever. The cat will come to expect the better, tastier, more expensive food, and will turn up its nose disdainfully at the cheaper brands of cat food from then on. The cat will actually **refuse** to eat the cheaper brand. Amazing. This will be your first inkling of the fact that your cat is a spoiled, willful child, and will demand - **demand** - the best in cat food.

Naturally, after demanding the best cat food money can by, it will then demand the best of **everything** money can buy for it - cat toys, cat carriers *(padded, catnipped, with a built-in live mouse to while away the hours being carried),* cat collars *(diamond-studded only, if you can even get one on the cat),* cat trees, even a cat bed. The cat will cease to be a slightly amusing pet/companion and will begin to be a serious drain on your weekly paycheck.

And it all starts with the right food. So, guys, be sure and choose carefully, as it's one of the few choices you'll get in your life with a cat. A nice dry cat food, crunchy and tasty, kept in one of those "perpetual" cat feeders so you don't have to bother opening a new can of wet cat food every day, and thus condition your cat to expecting the **best** in cat food. Your cat will assume that the dry cat food is its standard meal, and won't complain when she gets "Kitty Fare" bag o'cat food. Of course, a periodic special treat for your cat can also keep her in suspense and in line - some nice tuna fish or a gourmet cat food

("Gourmet" cat food? Who the hell ever thought up Gourmet cat food? Probably some half drunk General Foods rummy trying to save his job in the Animal Foods Group by coming up with a more expensive cat food that is actually the same as regular wet cat food, but

just costs more. Cat owners should have dealt with this threat in its early days by refusing to buy the stuff and by continuing to give their cats the same old dry food, but Nooooooo! You had to succumb to that old high-pressure advertising and think 'Well, Hell, just a nice once-in-awhile treat for my favorite cat.' Too bad, Buddy Roe, now you're stuck with the high-end cat food, and, oh, by the way -- that Porsche you were saving for? Forget it!)

6. Women

Food

No matter what you do, Men, when you invite your girlfriend over to your place for a nice dinner, **do not** give her food that is better than you eat yourself. If you do, you will spend the rest of your life regretting it. To a woman, Food is almost as important as Sex. Food is the base upon which the family unit is built. Food is what comes out of the kitchen, which is the domain of The Woman. A woman feels about food the way a man feels about sex. Proprietary. Exclusive. Restrictive. Food belongs to The Woman and is the second most important piece of ammunition in her female arsenal with which to snare a man for life. The first, of course, is sex - which is, of course, all we really want anyway. But if the way to a man's heart is under his stomach, the way to his agreeing to a marriage license is definitely through his taste buds and their repository.

The kitchen is the woman's special domain, and she will insist it be furnished to her exact specifications, with all appropriate foodstuffs and food preparation implements. Every item of cooking ware known to woman will eventually find its way into your/her kitchen. Many items will be completely incomprehensible and unrecognizable to you, unless you happen to be a Master Chef and a graduate of the Cordon Bleu Culinary Academy. In which case you'll never find a woman to live with, as women can't stand it when a man is a better cook than she is.

Anyway, in all normal instances, women will demand the best food and food preparation items money can buy. In short, The Woman will require The Man to furnish her with the best ingredients and foodstuffs, along with the best tools and utensils with which to prepare the food and the prettiest, most expensive plates and dishes and bowls and forks and knives and crystal with which to serve the food and drink.

Of course, Men, armed with this veritable cornucopia of food and things with which to prepare it and serve it, the woman will usually be able to whip up the most amazing array of meals you have ever seen or heard of. Next to Sex, Food is the thing which most attracts a man and keeps him around the house. Women know this and use it as one of their Primary Weapons (see Chapter 28).

Of course, as long as it tastes good and keeps us coming back for more, we're happy campers.

In short, Guys, you are screwed, blued and tattooed - right up against the wall. The Woman gets her way in the kitchen or you go back to munching on cold pizza and peanut butter sandwiches. Face it, Guys, women have total control over our eating habits once they get their hooks into us. Sex and food - two areas in which we are goners.

7. Cats

Curiosity

Okay, Men, you've been waiting patiently for this topic, so let's address it and get it out of the way. Everyone knows the old saying, "Curiosity killed the cat." Just because it's a platitude doesn't mean it isn't true. Of course it's true. That's why it's a platitude. The Curious Cat, sticking its nose or paw into places it doesn't belong - an electric socket, a barbecue grill, a running engine - will inevitably injure or kill itself. Of course, trying to get a cat **not** to be curious is pretty much impossible, so don't even attempt it. The Cat, by its very nature, **must** look into every nook and cranny and electric socket and doghouse of the neighbor's killer German Shepherd

(By the way, did you know that when these dogs were first imported to the US from Germany they were called Alsatian Wolf Dogs? True! Naturally, the dog-

loving public couldn't possibly adopt a cute and cuddly little puppy that might grow up and kill the family's youngest child, so the importers changed the name to German Shepherd - a much sweeter, more docile name. Marketing was already rearing its ugly head way back when.)

The Cat has no choice, it's in his nature, it's inbred, it's part of his inherent Catness. A non-curious cat would be like a tree-climbing dog - it just ain't possible. Of course, when the cat encounters something it would be better off not encountering, you would think it would cease being curious. Nope! Not a chance. Cats don't learn anything. Well, not for more than a few minutes, anyway. They only learn for the moment and then, the next hour or day they're right back trying to see what's down the rattlesnake hole. Can't help it, can't change it. Just hope the rattlesnake's asleep when the cat comes calling.

Pay attention here, Men. This is important, and understanding a cat's curiosity gene will help you immeasurably in understanding the exact same gene in women. Cats are wonderfully, surprisingly, relentlessly, unstoppably curious about their environment and about the creatures that inhabit it. Namely, mice, dogs, bugs and you. Cats can spend hours looking into paper bags (depending on size and depth). They are ecstatic when they find a new small dark place to explore, like under the bed or in a closet, or their idea of cat heaven - an attic. Their curiosity about electrical outlets is particularly endearing *(at least until they shove their paw into one and short-circuit all electrical appliances in the entire neighborhood, and fry themselves into catburgers at the same time.)*

Cats also dearly love those dangly Christmas-tree ornaments. They can swat at them for hours on end, and become rapturous when they are able to disengage one from the tree and bat it around the room and jump on it and then pretend they've never seen it after they leave it in the doorway for you to step on in your bare feet in the middle of the night when you're going for a drink of water.

And shoelaces! Be prepared to find frayed and chewed laces on your thousand-dollar Armani shoes. Your cat will amuse herself for days enjoying the culinary delights of Armani when you are away. Of course, she is never, never attracted to the laces on your old beat-up tennies, the ones that ceased to be valuable to anyone three years ago. Oh, No, only Armani and other prohibitively expensive shoes and laces, the ones that cost you two months' salary. Thank you, Gato!

Of course, he also makes up for these excursions into your wallet by being especially fascinated by your girlfriend's dangly earrings. Just let your date sit down on your sofa and The Cat will immediately make its presence known by soundlessly leaping up on the rear of the sofa and suddenly swatting at those irresistible earrings. Watch your date/girlfriend perform her own spectacular leap off the sofa when this happens. Judge the staying power of your date by her reaction to your cat. If your date begins to sneeze or back up fearfully against the door, or if she picks up your favorite lava lamp and chucks it at your cat, you know this will be your last date. Cats can help you judge a woman, so pay attention, Hoss.

8. Women
Curiosity

See Chapter 7 above.

Okay, I'll expand just a touch. Men, pay attention here, you really need to know this. A woman's curiosity, especially about her life's partner, is utterly and completely endless! A woman can not - CAN NOT - **ABSOLUTELY CAN NOT** - live with a man without continuously trying to discover every single thing about him. Every tiny little factoid, every event in his life, the name of every former girl friend, all about all of his relatives, the different cars he's owned, how he likes his roast beef cooked, which side of the bed he prefers, the name of his favorite baseball team when he was ten years old, the name of the first woman he slept with.

I honestly think this is an inborn trait in all women, which proves the thesis I advocate all throughout this book, i.e., that women are as curious as - if not more curious than - cats. All during the initial phases of a relationship, a woman will pry and wheedle and nudge each scrap of information out of her new partner, no matter how insignificant that information might be. Because the woman knows - and, Guys, you might as well accept this - that at some point in The Relationship she (the woman) will need access to some speck of information which she will use to attack us from an unforeseen direction, thus throwing us off balance and, hopefully, winning the argument. *(*Non sequitur *translates as "Never try to win an argument with a woman.")*

Women are absolutely insatiable when it comes to knowing everything about their partner. A woman is just not, and never can be, happy, until and unless she knows every single thing we have done and said in our life before we met her. Things we care little or nothing about assume gigantic proportions when digested by a woman. They must know, under penalty of being banned from *The Sisterhood of Women Everywhere*, things like what we do at work; how long we usually spend at the office; what our secretary looks like; the exact amount of our paycheck; balances and activity in our bank accounts. They question us endlessly, wearing us down until eventually, in sheer exhaustion, we give them the answers they want, just to get them to stop.

Endless curiosity. Women make cats look like indifferent couch potatoes. Women will question you about why you brought her flowers when it's not her birthday. About what you did every minute you were at that conference in Las Vegas. About why you've suddenly started looking at hairpieces. About where those red silk panties in your glove compartment came from *(This last is a tough one, Guys, so have a good explanation ready. Prepare, Prepare, just like for your work. "Gee, Dear, I promised Fred I wouldn't tell anyone, but he's become a cross-dresser and he didn't want his wife to find out so he left his red panties in my car." Or "Well, Honey, I just thought I'd see how it felt to wear women's silk undies for a change." Or, "What, those? Never saw them before. They must have been left there by the car's previous owner. Or the car salesman." Or, just possibly, "I needed something to clean the windshield during that big mudstorm last year, and I just grabbed something from a nearby trash can. Didn't even pay attention to what it was, just an old rag.")*

(Ed Note: Guys, no matter how much you want to finally submit and reveal the information the little woman wants, no matter how much she badgers you, for the sake of all future discussions and arguments, ***don't do it!*** *You'll be sorry. I guarantee it. Women,*

of course, count on their endless patience and perseverance to grind your resistance into the dust. They know you will almost always give up in the end. Her mother and grandmother and aunts and friends have all told her so. All she needs is to keep after you, pushing and prodding, slipping in her subtle questions and innuendoes, wearing you away, always grinding, grinding. She'll get what she wants in the end, she knows it. Even if she has to use both her penultimate and ultimate weapons: tears and the withholding of sex. [See Chapter 28].

(Men, fight against this last insidious inroad into your privacy and good memories for all you're worth. Don't let your woman have access to information she doesn't need to know. Lie, cheat, steal, joke about it, but never, never, let a woman know everything about you. You'll pay for it in the end. She'll ask seemingly innocent questions about how you learned how to use massage oil, or how you learned to give such great cunnilingus. If you answer her, thinking you're just showing her how much you love and trust her, she'll take all those little nuggets and jewels you give her and secrete them away in her little Future Argument Bag. Then, when the time is right for her and when you least expect it, she'll whip them out and completely disarm you in the middle of a discussion or an argument about some entirely different subject. As you stand there nonplused,

she'll smile smugly, cross her arms and leave the field of battle. Woman 1 - You 0. You lose again, Bud. You have been warned!)

Of course, as all men know, a woman's curiosity level, although seemingly inexhaustible, is actually highly selective. For example, a woman is never curious about changing the oil in her car and is amazed when the engine seizes up and the car needs a new engine. She is surprisingly uncurious as to why her checks bounce because her checking account has no money in it when there are still checks in her checkbook. She's never curious about all that emergency extra cash she finds in your underwear drawer. And she's especially never curious as to what things cost when she has a credit card. A woman's curiosity is definitely selective.

But, Men, what it comes down to overall is that women are, as noted previously, the more curious of the two human species. They'll never change, just like the cat. And, just like the cat, curiosity carried to the extreme will get them injured or killed. A woman **can not stand** not knowing everything there is to know about her chosen man. Her curiosity is virtually unquenchable. The more she can discover about us, the more she can store away that information for a day when she might need it. And that day will come, Men, you better believe it.

9. Cats
Mice and Other Gifts

Cats decide they should reward us poor humans from time to time with various gifts. Since the cat can't go down to Macy's and buy us a watch, they bring us dead things instead. Things they've killed with their own claws and teeth. Sometimes, of course, they're just hungry when they hunt and they decide to eat what they've killed. Other times they're just doing it for us, their human, the person who gives them gourmet cat food sometimes and scratches them under the chin. They just **know** we'll **love** a little dead bird or lizard or, if you live in the country, a little dead bunny rabbit.

Never forget how deadly the cat is. The cat is a hunter. The cat sleeps sixteen hours a day to be alert and vigilant and ready for the other eight hours when it is awake and hunting. The cat allows us to feed it and scratch it and it then thinks, "Well, what the hell, the human has been pretty good this month, why not kill something for him and bring it to him?" So you come home from a really crummy day at work and just want a stiff drink and a good steak, and what do you get on your favorite chair? Yep - a dead bird.

And, of course, the cat is hovering nearby, watching your reaction, meowing and checking out what you'll do with the wondrous present she's brought you. If you Yucch over it and grab a kitchen towel and pick up the unfortunate gift and chuck it into the trash, the cat will follow along and meow in its *"Don't you like it?"* voice. *"Hah? I got it just for you! It took me hours to stalk it and catch it and kill it, since I had to play with it awhile before I bit it in two. Hah, Human, whaddaya think? Isn't it great? Why are you throwing it into the big metal container along with the empty food boxes? Hah? Don't you like it?*

"Why, you ungrateful PERSON! Rowwrrr! I'm going out now, and I may or may not be back tonight and I may or may not forgive you for not appreciating my outstanding gift and I may or may not bring you another one next week, but I will if you really want me to......you do? You just had a really bad day and you really liked my gift? Is that why you're stroking me and getting out the gourmet cat food? Cool, Dude, next week a lizard!"

Cats know, somewhere in their tiny little cat brain, that we will eventually get tired of their other small tortures, like ripping our new drapes into long shreds, or killing every standing plant in the house with cat urine, so they choose the most opportune time to reinforce our affection for them - or for what they think is our affection for them. Actually, all they want is a warm cave and an endless supply of gourmet cat food. And they think that by bringing us what they consider a wonderful gift once in awhile, we will continue to supply their needs. And, of course, they're right, aren't they, Guys? Sure they are! A nice half-devoured mouse or lizard with bite marks covering its little inert body are just what the cat doctor ordered to keep us humans thinking kindly of The Cat. Yet another case of Feline Manipulation. Sound familiar, Guys?

10. Women

Flowers and other gifts

Most women love to get gifts, especially flowers and candy. Of course, when we do bring them gifts for no other reason than that we're thinking of them and want them to know how much we love them, their first *(OK, maybe second)* thought is always, "Uh, oh, what did you do now?" I mean, come on, all we want to do is please them and pet them and curry their favor, so they'll feel good and make us a nice dinner and give us sex and then leave us alone. Which is all we really want anyway, right, guys?

Why is it so difficult to give a woman a gift? Why are they always suspecting we have some ulterior motive? I mean, Jeez, it's been a really good day and we just want to share our success with them - or it's been a really rotten day and we need them to help cheer us up - or it's just been an ordinary day like all other days, but on the way home we pass one of the flower sellers on the corner and we think, "Well, Hell, just a nice once-in-awhile treat for my favorite woman." So you spring for a big bunch of red roses and you present them proudly to her when you find her cooking dinner and she Ooooohhs and Aaaahhhs and thanks you and then, sure as you're feeling better now, her eyes will narrow and her head will tilt slightly and she'll say, "OK, what did you do now?"

I mean, **come on**! Just a nice gesture on our part. Just because we want our woman to feel a little better than she's done all day, just because we want her to know how much we really do appreciate her and care for her -- and we get "What did you do now?" Well, **damn**! That's it for the flowers! Screw it! I'll go open my own damn bag of dry cat food and my own bottle of whiskey and have them alone in the study in front of the TV, where I should have gone in the first place, without any kitchen detours with an armload of cruddy flowers. Too bad, Buddy Roe - no welcome home kisses or pot roast for you. And, of course, no sex either, which is all you really wanted anyway.

And you know what, Men? It works the same with other gifts, no matter the value or size: jewelry, a new car, that little ceramic knick-knack she admired in the store last week. It really doesn't matter what the gift is, she just can not accept the fact that we're doing it out of love and affection rather than guilt. I mean, when a woman wants to give us a gift, her motives are (usually) pure and innocent, so why can't she think the same when the flowers are in the other hand? Hah? Come on, Gals, cut us some slack. We can be just as nice as you are, especially when we're feeling particularly horny and want a nice evening of good food and wine and sex - which is all we really want anyway.

So Women of the World, the next time your Man brings you a nice gift, accept it without reservation, put the flowers in a nice vase, fasten the necklace around your neck and admire it in a mirror, fling your arms around us and thank us profusely, and then fuck our brains out. That's all the thanks we really want anyway.

11. Cats

**Checking the House -
Because the attack can come at any time**

Anyone who has ever lived with a cat knows the frustrating experience of having the cat stand at the door and meow to go outside. We let them out, and, after about two minutes, there they are scratching at the door again, demanding to be let in. We let them in and, after about two or three minutes, there they are at the door again, demanding to be let out!

Jeez! What's with that? Well, guys, cats just **have** to check outside their cave enough times to satisfy themselves that there aren't any lurking dogs or wolves or other cats or any weird dangers out there so they can settle in for a good eight hours of sleep. Cats are funny that way. They need to assure themselves that it is safe to catch a few winks, and their genetic programming tells them the only way to do so is to check outside their cave several times before hunkering down for the night. Because the attack can come at any time!

You can't be too careful. That's why cats live so long. Or at least they did until cars came along.

12. Women
The 2 AM Talk -

Every man who has ever lived with a woman for any length of time has had it happen. At the most inopportune time of the night, a woman always "wants to talk."

"Honey? Are you awake? Honey? We need to talk, honey," she says seriously.

"What, now?" you answer groggily. "It's 2 AM and I've got an important meeting first thing in the morning and can't we wait on this until I get home tomorrow? Or next week? Or never?"

"**No!!**" in a petulant, whining voice. "It has to be **now**. I want to talk **now**! If you love me you'll wake up and talk to me. It's important!" *(push, push, shove, shove)*

Why women pick these strange times to talk to us about seemingly insignificant topics *(which, all of a sudden, right in the middle of a complaint about the broken screen door, morph unbelievingly into the much more serious, important topic of What's Wrong with the Marriage/Relationship)* is something men have been wondering and puzzling over for eons. What is so damned important that it can't wait until a more civilized time, like tomorrow after work? Why does it **have** to be in the middle of the damned night? Or right before the boss and his wife are due over for dinner? Or as you're walking out the door in the morning? Why does it **always** have to be **now**?

Well, guys, get ready for the answer. It was confided to me late one night *(when else?)* by a slightly inebriated woman friend who didn't really understand she was confiding the secret of the ages to a man. She told me directly and without blinking or flinching, just as if it was something I should have known. "No big deal, Bud, I thought you'd have known it all along, I just wanted to clarify it for you, maybe put it into simple words, which we women know you men have to have if you're ever to understand anything about us at all."

Oh, good, 2 AM and I'm getting Chapter One of The Standard Lecture. All I want to do is roll over and go back to sleep, or maybe cuddle for a little while. What I most definitely **do not** want to do is get into a deep, philosophical discussion about Our Relationship

The Feline Mystique

or be asked to tell her *Why I Really Love You* when I've just been awakened from a sound sleep and when I have to be up early for that damn meeting.

And "The Talk," as it usually turns out, is generally not all that big a deal - at least to us. It's **always** something that could easily have waited until tomorrow, or the next day -- or never. Why do women always seem to want reassurance about the relationship or the kids or her career or why you forgot to bring home some bread the other day at such odd times? Are you ready for this, Guys?

Because the attack can come at any time!

Yep, you got it. A woman's middle-of-the-night talk is the cat's equivalent of checking outside the cave for possible dangers, intruders, large animals, dragons, marauding humans, runaway buses, etc. The subject of The Talk doesn't really matter at all. A woman's genetic programming demands that she constantly require our reassurance that we are there - awake, armed, vicious, on guard - to protect her at any time of the day or night, because The Attack Can Come at Any Time. That's it!

Understand that, and you will be able to wake up all the way and listen to her monologue and then spend a few serious minutes reassuring your woman that all is OK and that you love her and cherish her and will always be there to protect her, at any time of the day or night. You're zealously guarding the cave and no wild animals or other enemies intent on kidnap and rape will get into the cave. You're on the job, armed with your urban assault rifle, awake or asleep, ready to leap up and wield your sword and slay the invading dragon. *(Ed Note: mixed metaphors are my specialty)*

Just take a few minutes to reassure her. Listen to what she says, agree with her, nod now and then, look her in the eye and assure her that you **do** love her and that you will **always** be there for her and that your relationship is the most important thing in the world to you, even more important than the meeting the next morning. Make sure she knows you care and will protect and cherish her always. Then maybe she'll give you some "Thank You Sex," which, of course, is all we really want anyway. After which you can go back to sleep.

13. Cats
Love and Sex

Sex between more-or-less consenting adult cats is not a fun affair - at least for the female. In fact, it is downright painful for the female, as the male cat has a barbed penis. Rather wickedly barbed, actually, and not like those rubbery little barbs on the French Ticklers you can get in gas station vending machines. So the female yowls and screams and growls at the male, but she puts up with it because her genetic programming tells her she has to do this to procreate her species. When the male cat is finished grunting and growling over her and biting her on the neck and lower back, the female immediately shakes him off and goes her own way again.

Then when the kittens are ready to be born, the female seeks the safest place she can find to have them. I once had a cat give birth in the box of Christmas-tree ornaments stored on top of the beams in the garage. At least that gave me an excuse to buy new ornaments the next year - no more of those damn antique angels for the top of the tree - from then on it was cool stars and pointy shiny Guy Things. Much better.

Anyway, Momma Cat won't let the male cat anywhere near her kittens for several days or weeks, depending on when she deems them able to take care of themselves. Until then, Men, keep away! Maternity has reared its ugly head and things will never be the same again.

The cat is a night animal, hunting and prowling and yowling and loving and gathering in cat groups at night. It's when they do their best work. You'll be trying to get to sleep and you'll hear that strange, mournful yowl in the darkness out behind the garage. If you're attuned to your cat, you'll undoubtedly recognize it as the male's version of the *"C'mere, Kitty, Poppa wants some lovin"* yowl.

Of course, no matter how closely you (or the female cat) listen, there's no meow or yowl or hint about that wickedly barbed penis. Male cats know even an otherwise tractable female cat would balk if shown that nasty tool. So they keep it sheathed until the female is belly-down and butt-high and is in female cat heaven by being bitten on the neck and lower back by Mr. Tom, and then he slips her the magic wand covered with barbs and thorns. That's what all that yowling is late at night out by the garbage cans: the female cat's yowl saying *"Get that damn torture stick away from me, Mr. MacCavity, or at least make it quick. Who ever said male cats were good lovers?"*

14. Women
Love and Sex -- Claws and Scratching

Sex between consenting adult humans is - or should be - a wonderful experience. At best, it often ends up extremely painful for the man because the woman has sharp fingernails and teeth. But at least most men don't have a barbed penis *(unless they try out those new French ticklers they found in the men's room of their favorite service station)*.

However, sex is a primary motivator in selecting a mate, for which men are eternally grateful and woman are eternally neutral. OK, some women actually enjoy sex, and like to have it often when entering into a new relationship. Over time, however, and especially after the man has made the relationship permanent *(by supplying house, car, clothes, kitchen utensils, etc)*, and really especially after the first child is born, the woman often loses the sense of urgency which used to imbue her sexual appetites. At which point men often develop the old Seven Year Itch and start looking around for a sexual surrogate. Or buy one of those inflatable sex dolls. Whatever. At any rate, we men then know we have years and years to live with this woman we married without the possibility of lots and lots of sex. Which is, of course, all we really wanted anyway.

So, let's get this clear once and for all: Men require sex at all times and in all places, whenever they happen to be in the mood. At the dinner table, over the breakfast coffee, in the car on the way to work, when a woman bends over to get a pot from a kitchen cabinet, in the shower, while the woman is pondering her dress selection for the day. But not, of course, while watching football on TV. Except, maybe, at half-time.

Women, on the other hand, have great sex drives while they're single and dating and trying to land a man. This marvelous sex drive, which easily hooks us and reels us in, continues unabated right up until the kids start to come, at which time the woman's maternal instincts take over, and sex becomes a matter of planning and the right timing. At least until the kids are old enough to fend for themselves. Women seem to enjoy sex as much as men before commitment and marriage, after which sex becomes secondary to them, taking back seat to a good cave and money, the ability to protect the home and cave, kids, food, a nice car, jewelry, flowers. After commitment, a woman need gifts to get her kick-started for sex. Men, of course, are walking erections, and can and do want sex anywhere, anytime. Hey, we worked for this luxurious cave and nice car and cool furniture and great jewelry and we provided all this good stuff and we gave you your kids, now we want our just desserts. Sex. Anywhere, anytime.

So, Guys, keep this in mind. Too many women view sex as a mildly pleasurable activity designed to snare a mate and to have children. Other than that, they can usually take it or leave it. Kids and home come first, their primary concerns. Nesters. Gotta have that perfect nest.

15. Cats
Yowling

Cats talk to us all the time. They have a very distinctive vocabulary, if you just learn how to recognize it. The cat's meows and yowls and purrs all signify something to the cat, and they give it their best shot trying to communicate with us. Cat language is sort of like Chinese, in that it depends upon tone to get its meaning across. The cat has developed a variety of tones for its meows and yowls which, to the cat, are perfectly clear in meaning. It just remains for us humans to pay attention and listen closely and carefully to the cat. The meaning is there and it's clear if we just take the time to study and hear it. When you live with a cat for any length of time, you should be able to eventually differentiate between its variety of meows and yowls. Because cats have a whole series of differently-toned yowls. Included in the Cat's repertoire of yowls are:

The "Hi, Human, you're finally home and I'm hungry" yowl.

The "Let me out of the house so I can check for danger" yowl.

The "Let me back in the house, it's safe out here" yowl.

The "Look what I brought you this time" yowl.

The "Get off my back you stupid male cat with the barbed penis" yowl (Female cat).

The "Hey, baby, wanna party?" yowl (Male cat).

The "Hi, sailor, new in town and do you want to stroke me and chuck my chin and scratch my head for awhile?" meow.

The "If you won't let me out of the house to take a crap I'm using your new philodendron" yowl.

The "Hey, Bud, check out this great mouse-head I brought you," meow.

The "Cat crap in your philodendron? Not me, must have been the dog," meow.

Pay attention, guys! Your cat is talking to you! Even more expressive than its domesticated counterpart, the dog, the cat is able to communicate with its human roommates through an entire series of meows and yowls. It's all in the tone, men. Get it? The tone. Just listen, stretch those auditory muscles and you can hear what your cat is telling you. Cats are extremely expressive (witness their "philodendron" yowl), and will always give you the perfect yowl to let you know exactly what they want. You just have to listen.

16. Women

The Female Equivalent of Yowling

Now, a woman's yowls, or differences in tones of voice, are also distinctive and we must learn to recognize their meanings if we are to survive our time with them. This is extremely important, Men. You will not last past the first week if you cannot interpret your woman's different yowls and whines and wheedles and tones of voice. Women are not like us, Guys. They are devious and sneaky, and they can't just come right out and say what they mean. They have to use a tone of voice which, they assume, we, as their Man, will be able to interpret correctly and therefore we will be able to understand everything they don't say, underneath everything they do say.

Understanding a woman's tone of voice is critical to understanding a woman. No matter what you do to please your woman, it will never be enough, and it will never be right, unless you understand what it is she's really saying. Men, give this book to your five-year-old son so he can begin practicing immediately. It's never too soon to start, even if you've never considered this area before now. Give your kid the benefit of your experience. Young boys should start learning how to interpret a young girl's tones of voice as soon as possible, all the better to be able to deal with older girls.

So, Guys, if you spend lots of time up front listening to a woman's yowls and whines and tones of voice, you'll reap the rewards when you're older and ready to share your life with a woman. Women count on us not being able to understand their tones of voice, and they use this weapon against us whenever it pleases them, just to keep us off balance and drive us crazy. Being able to grasp their meanings will put you miles in front of them and will enable you to stomp on any argument or potential misunderstanding before it gets off the ground. So, Guys, here we go.

First, and most important (to the woman, anyway) is the "Honey, I need some money to go shopping" yowl.

Then there's the "Get your own damn dinner, I need some Me Time" yowl.

The "If you buy me that beautiful bracelet in the window I'll let you have sex with me" meow.

The Feline Mystique

The "If you **don't** buy me that beautiful bracelet in the window I **won't** let you have sex with me" yowl.

The "OK, just for awhile, but I really do have a headache" yowl.

The "Well, if you don't know what you did I'm not going to tell you" (**really** frustrating!) yowl.

The "Do you think I'm fat?" meow/whine?

And, of course, the "Get the fuck away from me you hairy, heavy-handed ape" PMS yowl. We all know that one really well, don't we Guys?

A few lesser yowls, whines and whimpers are also included in the woman's Yowl Arsenal, such as:

The "Honey, can you come here and keep me company? I'm lonely," piteous meow

The "Honey, can you get me some peanut butter ice cream? I'm hungry," (pregnant) meow

The "Honey, can you take out the trash?" meow

17. Cats

Cuddling, Petting and Stroking, Chin-Chucking, Biting, Sharpening Claws and Rubbing the Wrong Way

How do you stroke a cat? Carefully, softly, gently, but firmly. Scratch it lightly under its chin, from throat to chin. Scratch between its ears, then a long, soft stroke down its back to the spot just above its tail, where you can give it a good firm scratching. Female cats especially love this spot, as it's right where the male cat bites her to get her to have sex with him. Male cats, understandably, get somewhat peeved if you scratch this spot, as they dislike being mistaken for a female.

Never, ever, rub cats the wrong way - literally and figuratively. Cats are very specific about the ways in which they like to - prefer to - **demand to** - be stroked and cuddled. They'll let you know if you're doing it wrong. A small bite on the webbing of the hand between the thumb and forefinger; a quick scratch down the leg, bringing just the right amount of blood; an annoyed, *"Hey, Bud, do it right or I'll spray your last cashmere sweater!"* yowl.

Of course, if you stroke a cat the correct way, you'll be rewarded with a buzzing sound that humans interpret as a "purrrrrrrr." This is a good thing, as it means you are stroking the cat the right way and the cat is happy and is letting you know it. If you continue your cat-pleasing strokes, and listen very carefully, in fact, you will hear the cat actually saying, "purrrrrr-fect!"

The cat usually loves to be stroked and petted. She will let you know this by rubbing up against you, head-butting you, rubbing her head under your hand in a sort of self-petting movement. The cat wants attention, and she wants it NOW, Human! If you're reading a book or watching a football game, you had better take notice and at least give the cat some perfunctory strokes, lest he spray your bowl of popcorn when you aren't looking. Of course, a few involuntary strokes will usually lead to a full-blown Caress-a-thon, during which the cat will roll over and demand strokes and massages and some really heavy-duty scratching and chin-chucking. Be prepared, Guys. The Cat knows what she wants and how to make us give it to her. The cat is manipulative and sneaky in this way. Sound familiar?

The Feline Mystique

So, men, if uncertain as to how to scratch a cat, pick up a cat book and learn how to do it right. Read up on stroking technique and style and the location of the cat's erogenous and sensitive zones. Better get it right the first time. Or suffer the consequences.

18. Women

Cuddling, Petting and Stroking, Chin-Chucking, Biting, Sharpening Claws and Rubbing the Wrong Way

Men need women for sex. That's right, guys - and gals - now it's out in the open. OK, we say we want love and affection and a home and children and all the other supposedly normal things society has been telling us we're supposed to have ever since around 4,000 Before the Common Era, in order to ensure the continuance of the race. But, and we're being honest now, what we really want women for is sex. Plus, of course, a housekeeper who will pick up after us and fix us some food once in awhile, and generally keep our cave free of nasty used animal parts. If they're nice enough to throw in a six-pack of beer and a football game on TV, well, we'll let them hang around for awhile. As long as, once the football game is over, we can have sex with them. Which is all we really want anyway.

We do prefer our women to be willing participants in the sexual Olympics, of course, as we realize women have their own needs - like a nice home/cave, children, labor-saving appliances and, obviously, a man to provide all these things. See, guys, women are genetically programmed to want one man to provide for them. The strongest, best man they can find. The Herd Bull. Because, face it, with only a few exceptions down the centuries, women are not hunter-gatherers. They are cave-cleaners and kid-bearers. So they want all these things that usually only a man can provide.

But they also know, somewhere down deep in their genes *(or in their jeans, if it comes to that),* that the price they have to pay is sex. Usually the price is minimal and often even enjoyable, but it's still the price. Sometimes they pay it gladly, willingly, and sometimes grudgingly, but pay it they must. Unfortunately for the relationship between the sexes, however, women take sex much more seriously than do men. See, to men, sex is gym; to women, it's church. Men engage in sex as sport and enjoy the game as long as they are able and capable. Find an attractive woman, woo her and win her (which means getting her into bed), then say "Thank You, Dear," and move on. Women, on the other hand, see sex as The C Word - commitment. As soon as they have allowed us to have sex with them, women begin planning the wedding and start looking at china patterns.

Along the way, of course, as every man knows, women also want to change us into whatever it is they think they want in their ideal man. Unfortunately for women, we are not interested in change. We want things exactly as they were when we first met and had sex with our woman. Change is O - U - T. We just want food and sex, and not necessarily in that order.

And, quite naturally *(and even though we've covered this area previously, it's still a good idea to remember it and repeat it again),* due to our genetic programming, once we've had sex and children and a house and garden tools with one woman, we need to seek out another woman with whom to have some more sex. Men are sexual beasts, as feminists so often tell anyone who will listen to their inane ramblings. We need women to satisfy our basic need. Which is sex. Keep in mind, guys and gals, that the male lion will, given the chance, kill the newborn cubs in order to have sex with the female again. OK, so we haven't quite gotten to that place yet, have we guys? But women will never be quite certain that we haven't!

OK, so anyway, the subject of this chapter, Stroking a Woman. Women have at least 173 sensitive areas on their bodies, lots more than men, who really have only one. On women they are called erogenous zones, or "feel-good spots." Figure out how to stroke a woman correctly and you'll get a low-throated "Mmmmmmmmmm" out of her. Raising the bar, kiss just the right spot on her body and get a gasp of quickly-indrawn breath followed by a long drawn-out "Ooooooooohhhhhhh." Move your stroking and nibbling up a notch, into the realm of sensuousness, and be rewarded with an astonishingly feline "Purrrrrrrrr." See, guys, women really are like cats.

Men don't require much in the way of foreplay to get ready for sex. Actually, just the sight of a bare breast or rounded bottom will set most men off immediately. Rarin' to go, that's the typical Guy. Many men will get excited at merely hearing certain suggestive words; in fact, the word "moist" is able to cause a large number of men to have an immediate erection and even, in some extreme cases, orgasm.

Women, on the other hand (as usual), require lots and lots of foreplay before they are ready for sex (or, in the male lexicon, when they are "moist"). So it behooves us men to read a few books and magazine articles on the proper way to please a woman before attempting to enter into a relationship with one. *Cosmo* is especially good at preparing a man for this phase of his life. Its articles contain all sorts of fun instructions on *How to Satisfy Your Woman.* Men can easily learn the locations of all of a woman's "feel-good spots," and, with just a little study and reading, can find out how to give a woman the greatest pleasure.

Stroking, petting, caressing, massaging, fondling - women react strongly to all of these activities and will become putty in your hands if you can master the proper stroking techniques. Like the cat, a woman will offer her back to be massaged and stroked using some warm massage oil. She will then roll over and present her front for more stimulating attention. In fact, Guys, if you can master the erotic potential of an oiled feather, or a silver teaspoon, or a strawberry, you can pretty much have anything you want from your woman - or, for that matter, your cat.

Stroking a woman? Always rub them the right way; if you rub them the wrong way, you're in deep doo-doo.

19. Cats

Laughing at a Cat

Oooooohhh, don't **ever** laugh at your cat! The cat is the haughty mistress of all she surveys. The cat can do anything: jump upward five times its length; hunt and catch small forest animals; walk precariously along a one-inch ledge 50 feet above the ground; climb the stoutest tree *(or sofa, or drapes)*. The cat does all these things with a supercilious, better-than-thou aloofness that can easily batter down even a strong man. The cat is indestructible and wonderful. The cat is perfect.

So, when the cat slips off your fireplace mantle and lands on the hot hearth and immediately leaps off yowling its indignancy *(the "It wasn't me, it was my evil twin Skippy" yowl)*, well, the cat is astounded that its perfection has been proven less than perfect. The cat will quickly look around to see if anyone - human being, another cat or, worst of all, the family dog - has seen its humiliation. You may even hear a quiet *"You didn't see that, did you?"* meow.

And if we do happen to witness its embarrassment, and we do happen to be unable to stifle a laugh at the Perfect Cat's mistake, well, don't expect the cat to speak to you for at least three days. The wounded cat's hurt expression and tiny yowl *(the "OK for now, Buddy Roe, but next time you slip on the ice and crash to the ground, I'll be there to snicker at you!" yowl)* will trail it as it slinks away to hide for awhile until it recovers from its embarrassing episode. And by the way, Men, that new $500 Armani tie you wanted to wear to work tomorrow? It won't look too good in the morning covered with cat spray.

20. Women

Laughing at a Woman

You do so at your own risk, my friend. If you value your testicles and want to keep them intact and damage-free, NEVER laugh at your woman. You have been warned.

Never forget, women need constant reassurance - about everything! Given that women have the one thing that all (straight) men want, they are remarkably insecure about themselves. Thus, they are always seeking reassurance for whatever they do and say, and whatever they (think) they look like.

"Honey, do you think I look fat?," she'll ask, while standing naked in front of the full-length bedroom mirror, twisting and turning every which way to see if she can find just the tiniest wrinkle of extra flesh somewhere on her perfect body. Once again, Men, if you want dinner that night, and if you want to keep the peace in the apartment, and especially if you want to keep on getting sex, you will answer, immediately and automatically, without hesitation and without even thinking about it, "Oh, no, dear, you are absolutely perfect, not an ounce of additional flesh on you anywhere, your body is just as trim and slim as the day we met; in fact, I think you should consider doing some modeling for Ralph Lauren clothes."

Naturally, you will spout these memorized words no matter what she looks like, whether she only weighs 97 pounds dripping wet and holding a stick of butter in each hand, or if she has thighs that could double as tree trunks. If she has a cute bubble butt that can crack walnuts, so much the better: firm and trim and perfectly round. Compliment her on her girlish figure. Because, Guys, the "Honey, I'm not fat, am I?," question is unanswerable. Especially if you hesitate in answering for even half a second. No hesitation, Men. The fact that you stop to think and ponder and consider and check her out means, to her, that she should audition for the job of Fat Lady in the circus!

Never, never, never snicker or hoot or snort or chuckle or laugh in any way, shape or form when you get asked this question (and you will, Guys, believe it!). What *to us* is an indication of complete unbelief that our woman - possessor of The World's Most Perfect

Body - would even think of asking us such a question is, *to her,* a stake through her heart. She now knows you definitely think she's a porker and will be trading her in on a newer, slimmer model within the week. Those sleek thighs take on the appearance of wrinkled, cellulite-covered bridge supports. Her well-muscled and tanned arms are now gross Pillsbury Doughboy appendages. That perfectly-rounded derriere is now a pair of hanging hams.

No laughing, Guys. Check the language in the above paragraphs, learn it, memorize it and use it as needed, without hesitation, but with earnestness and gusto and complete conviction. If you are convincing, she'll swivel toward you and give you the best afternoon sex of your life. Which is all we really want anyway.

21. Grooming
Cats

Cats clean themselves constantly. Humans refer to it as grooming. Cats do this because they want to ensure the next victim of their hunt has no chance to smell the dried blood and other detritus from their previous victims on their claws, fur, breath and teeth. Cats groom themselves for much of the time they are awake - say, six of the eight hours. They are fastidious in that they want to be sure they can sneak up on an unsuspecting victim and thereby ensure they will be able to attack, capture, play with and finally dispatch their victim without the victim knowing they are anywhere in the vicinity. If the cat is not sparkling clean, there will be no supper tonight. The slightest hint of an odor of spoiled or rotten or undigested meat will be enough to send the cat's next potential victims scurrying for the skies or holes.

Constant grooming is the cat's mantra. Grooming keeps the cat quiet and occupied and is inbred in the cat to the point of obsessiveness. If you have a pair of cats, they will usually groom each other as well as themselves, getting those hard-to-reach places, and at the same time making the female cat think the male cat is an okay guy and doesn't really have a barbed penis, like her mother told her, and even if he did, how much could it really hurt.....

The cat's grooming is so important, in fact, that cats are genetically furnished with a sandpapery tongue, the better to get all those little bits of nastiness off the cat's fur and claws. Social grooming is such an important part of a cat's life, in fact, that the cat will also include you, the human, in its ministrations, the better to show you its acceptance of you into the cat tribe. Cats love to groom, and will spend hours at it. "Om Mane Padme Om, I'm a Cat and I love to Groom."

22. Grooming
Women

Ah, now, women. In order to ensure their success in their hunt for a mate/sexual partner, women spend the same amount of time on grooming as do cats: about eight hours a day. But a woman's approach to grooming is radically different from the cat's. The cat seeks to divest itself of all odors and aromas and smells. Women, on the other hand, absolutely drench, slather, douse, layer, cover, immerse themselves in a veritable ocean of liquids, lotions, powders, creams, sprays, perfumes, balms and unguents.

Not a single solitary hint of a natural smell or odor - of their own or of any previous conquest's - stands even the slightest chance of getting through all the smells and aromas and layers of the modern woman's grooming essentials. After all, nothing resonates on a woman's skin, nothing oozes out of a woman's pores, nothing permeates the very air around her, like the remnants of a stale relationship.

For a man, soap and water fill the cleanliness and grooming bill. And maybe a swipe or two of deodorant. Women spend thousands of dollars a year on grooming "essentials" - soaps, lotions, powders, douches, perfumes, toe creams, nail polishes, hair spray, undie drawer sachets, hair removers, et cetera, ad infinitum. Grooming for a woman is almost as critical as for a cat, and she will, like the cat, spend hours at it.

She will start preparing for an evening out at least two days before it is time to leave, and when time to leave comes around she still won't be ready. No matter how perfect she looks to us, no matter that we think she's ready to pose for a Playboy centerfold, she will continue to find some uncovered blemish or spot, some patch of skin not inundated with creams and lotions, some unwanted tiny blonde hair growing almost unnoticed and forgotten behind her ear.

Get used to it, Men. Watching the cat groom itself (and others), sitting patiently in your recliner with a beer and the football game blasting away, will help prepare you for the endless grooming preparations a woman has to go through before she can leave the house. So no matter what time you have to leave for the party or theater, you always know you will have at least 30 more minutes to have yet another beer or to watch just a little bit more of the playoffs before she is ready to go. This is the way it has always been, the way it is, and the way it will always be, forever and ever, world without end, amen.

23. Cats

Domesticity - Housebreaking the Cat

Once the Cat has settled into its new home, the home becomes hers. No question about it. The Cat allows you, the Man, to share her space with her, just as long as you continue to give her food and scratch her under the chin once in awhile.

Cats will see their new abode as their cave, but as far as housebreaking the cat, doubtful, Guys, very doubtful. The best you can hope for is that the cat will learn to use the litter box if an inside cat or the cat door if an outside cat - which cats prefer. They'd rather leave their scat outside than have it hanging around in their cave with them. Cats are fastidious roommates, after all, given half a chance. And BTW, Men, do not even think about de-clawing your cat and friend. That's like tearing out a human's fingernails. Torture. Besides, it leaves the cat defenseless. Not a nice thing to do. If you worry abut claw damage to your drapes and sofas, you shouldn't have a cat in the first place.

One of the more unfortunate results of domesticating a cat is the change in its hunting skills. Ever watch a cat capture and then proceed to "play with" a bird or mouse or lizard or goldfish it intends to eat? This is the domestic cat's way of finalizing and ritualizing its hunt. House cats instinctively bat around a captured mouse before tiring of the game and ripping the mouse to shreds and devouring it. See, the cat has to go through this playing/batting/fiddling process in order to reach its foregone conclusion: mouse dinner.

Upon capturing the mouse, the cat will carry its prey to a safe corner of the house where it will then release the poor unfortunate creature. Said creature will then, naturally, think the cat has screwed up and will try to escape. The creature won't see the cat's paws whip around and bat the mouse back into the corner. Mousie is lunch, but doesn't know it, and it will continue trying to escape. The cat, naturally, will continue to contain the mouse within its sphere of influence for as long as the cat's instinct (and patience) tells it to, at which time the cat will tire of the game and will sit down to a tasty dinner of mouse parts.

Cat psychologists say this behavior in domestic cats is actually a manifestation of the hunting activities of wild cats. In other words, since the house cat gets all the food it wants from its roommate (You, Bozo!), it really doesn't need to hunt. But - the cat's instinct still says "Hunt!," so when the cat bags a small creature that has encroached on its domain, the hunt reflex is triggered in the form we humans see as "playing with its food." The cat enjoys this activity/play immensely, as it reminds him, somewhere deep down in his little cat brain, that his ancestors were mighty hunters and, if placed in the wild, he, too, could easily assume this ancient role again with minimal transition time. "Playing" will quickly revert to hunting and the cat will be complete again.

24. Women

Domesticity - Housebreaking a Woman

Once the woman has claimed her new home for herself, it then belongs to her forevermore, ever after, ad infinitum, ad nauseum. She may allow us poor men to live there with her, and to make the money with which to buy the furniture for her, and to pay the mortgage, and to mow the lawn and pull the weeds, but the house, the cave, really belongs to her. It is her property.

The woman is happy with her cave and her food. She is a Nester, not a Hunter. So, Guys, the domestic human female rarely ever sinks to the level of playing with her food; however, if you watch her closely you will be able to observe behavior which is directly analogous *(at least according to the author)*. Men are, at first, amused by this behavior, and then, later, annoyed and frustrated and impatient. The behavior in question, of course, is what we men see as "Fiddling," and what women undoubtedly see as "Arranging my world to my satisfaction."

Any semi-observant male will attest, in a court of law, that women are inveterate Fiddlers. They are always touching and arranging and rearranging and moving things and performing all sorts of needless little physical tasks with their hands. Women are tactile creatures, and in order to feel at home in an otherwise hostile environment *(and every woman since the beginning of time has known that the world is a hostile environment!)*, they must exercise their unique brand of control over their world by fondling and touching and manipulating. Physically, intellectually and emotionally. Witness the housewife's two primary activities: cleaning and cooking.

Cleaning the house/cave is of critical importance to a woman. She just can not feel truly happy or at peace unless her abode is completely and utterly sterile and free of dust, dirt, long-deceased insects, soiled clothes and muddy foot prints. Another genetic program? Possibly. Oh, hell, probably! Notice how exhaustedly happy and smiling a woman is after she's vacuumed and dusted and swiped and cleaned and watered the plants for a few hours? Now she's ready for a long, hot bath with perfumed suds and then a nice relaxing glass of wine and some cheese and crackers. Sex? With her man?

Happy and sated as she is from a morning of cleaning? Not a chance, Boys. Domesticity effectively removes most of the sexual desire from a woman. Cleanliness is the domesticated woman's beginning and ending, her clean cave, her shout to the world that her cave is now the cleanest and most spotless one around and you can come in and see for yourself, you nosy parker neighbor. So there, nyah, nyah, nyah.

Plus, a woman also has to know - **really has to know** - just where everything is in her house. She must be in complete and total control of her environment, and that means knowing where all of her personal property is at every moment and how to get to it if she needs it. Even down to and including the nose-hair remover you bought her as a gag gift for her last birthday. She'll never, ever use it, but she always has to know just where it is. Just in case.

For example, when you're tired of rummaging around in your tie drawer for that really cool Perry Ellis tie she bought you last Christmas, and you yell downstairs, "Honey? Where's my red and yellow Perry Ellis tie?," she immediately yells back, "Check the spare sock drawer under the winter underwear." Yep, there it is. How does she do it? She has no choice, it's built into her genetic coding. Control over her environment. It's why she hates cars and escalators.

Still not convinced, Guys? Okay, next time the opportunity presents itself *(and it will be sooner than you think),* watch a woman (1) in line at the supermarket checkout counter, and (2) getting into a car preparatory to driving away. You simply can not miss the amazing gyrations women go through in these inimical *(to them, anyway),* situations.

(1) At The Supermarket

The woman has filled her shopping cart with her and her family's edible and hygienic goodies, and she is ready for the upcoming week's meals and cleaning and personal hygiene. She gets in line at a checkout counter and patiently pushes her cart forward an inch at a time as the women in front of her go through their own unique Fiddling techniques. When the time comes for her to empty her cart, she is ready. Purse firmly closed and latched and hanging from her shoulder and clasped firmly between her arm and side, she begins to unload her basket, placing each item one by one onto the cashier's conveyor belt.

One by one. One item at a time. Meticulously and patiently and robot-like. Bend down, pick up an item, straighten up, rotate arm and hand clutching item over the conveyor belt, release item, repeat, repeat, ad infinitum, or at least until all of the items have been successfully transferred from the basket to the conveyor belt. *(Ed Note: If you ever happen to observe a woman twitching when she is asleep, this is what she is dreaming about as her fingers open and close and twitch and grasp).*

Finally, she's next. She focuses her hawk-like gaze on the computer as the checker scans every item, verifying the price on the tag against what the computer flashes after reading the bar code. Her purse is still clutched firmly between arm and side, tightly closed. At long last, the checker asks, "Anything else?" "No, thank you," the woman answers. The checker looks at her computer and says, "That'll be sixty-two dollars and seventy-five cents." And it is NOW, all of you Well-Organized and Well-Prepared Men Everywhere, that the fun begins.

Looking like she has never been to the supermarket before, and has never even contemplated the possibility that she might actually have to hand over money for her goodies, the woman's eyes widen as a sudden thought stabs her in the brain: *"I have to pay for all this stuff. Oh! How do I do that? What do I need? Aaaahhh, of course, money. But wait - where is my money? Why, where else, of course, it's in my wallet. And where is my wallet? Why, in my purse. Which is hanging from my shoulder. Closed. I need my money!"* You can almost see - almost touch - almost feel her thoughts as they slog patiently, slowly, doggedly through her mind. We men, standing behind the woman, watch in stupefied and rather impatient amazement as the woman goes into her act.

"Ladies, grab your purses. It's time for *The Checkout Line Dance!*"

'Well, open up your purse real wide,
Now it's time to look inside.
Rummage through it, what's in there?
Lipstick, car keys, spray for hair.
'Take things out and close the flap,
How did I get all this crap?
Where the hell's my wallet now?
Oh, look, there's my tampax - Wow!
'Do se do and dig right in,
There's that long lost pint of gin.
Ah, here's my wallet, at long last,
Guess I better pay real fast.
'Behind me, people in the line,
Now aren't feeling quite so fine.
They're watching me with evil glares,
I could be injured by their stares.
'Unsnap the wallet, open it now,
Turn around and take a bow.

The Feline Mystique

Take out some money, count it slow
Hey, I'm a Woman, don't'cha know?
'Okay, I've got all the bills,
Now I need some downer pills.
Let's see, how much change is here?
Just enough, so have no fear.
'Count each coin and set them down,
The cashier's giving me a frown.
But now I've paid it, it's okay,
I'll live to shop another day.'
Burma Shave

Whew! Above the ringing of the cash register (finally!) can be heard the gnashing of teeth by all of the men in line behind the clueless woman. It is truly a wonder that any woman ever gets out of the supermarket checkout line alive. Of course, this is only the first part of The Payment Ritual. Part Two consists of the woman getting her change and putting all the coins and bills back into her wallet, each coin and bill placed one at a time into its proper receptacle, then closing the wallet, putting the wallet back into the purse, slinging purse over shoulder, taking a deep breath and letting it out, sighing mightily, turning and marching smartly out of line, leaving every man behind her stupefied with amazement, pissed beyond belief, and ready to scurry back to exchange the melted ice cream for a new container with still-frozen contents. Thus endeth the woman's sojourn to the supermarket.

(2) Getting in the Car

As a woman approaches a car, which, don't forget, is a machine used to transport people, kids, dogs and groceries from one place to another, does she begin searching in the black hole of her purse for her keys? Does she hell! Women seem genetically incapable of preparing for any activity until the final instant when action is actually needed (See "At the Supermarket" above). This truism is especially evident when a woman is preparing to use a car.

After spending a minimum of five minutes standing next to the car searching for her car keys in the bottomless pit of her purse, she finally emerges triumphant, clutching the car keys in a hand stained blue by the leaking souvenir pen she put in there in 1987 and hasn't used since. She manages to open the car door and then does that peculiarly female side/slide entry into the driver's seat. Be warned, Men, another Fiddle Dance is about to begin. The steps are choreographed especially for the woman driver:

Ready for the *Let's Go For A Drive* Olympics?

1. Adjust skirt
2. Drop car keys onto floor of car
3. Move rear-view mirror up infinitesimally
4. Grope on floor for car keys
5. Can't find keys. Damn! Call girlfriend on cell phone re: tonight's party
6. Try to turn on radio
7. Ooops, need keys for that!
8. Pat hair into place
9. Finally locate car keys
10. Apply lipstick
11. Adjust skirt
12. Drop car keys again
13. Give under-the-breath curse while feeling for keys
14. Kick off shoes
15. Find keys, insert key into ignition slot
16. Key won't turn. Remove key and stare at it for 37 seconds exactly
17. Realize it is trunk key
18. Find ignition key after three tries and turn on engine
19. Move rear view mirror down infinitesimally
20. Adjust seat belt

21. Adjust bra straps
22. Turn on radio
23. Check side view mirror
24. Adjust side view mirror infinitesimally
25. Wipe off lipstick and try another shade
26. Adjust skirt
27. Make one last all-around check to ensure all tasks have been carried out to her satisfaction.
28. Adjust rear view mirror upwards one last time
29. Check hair and makeup in visor mirror
30. Turn on windshield wipers to clean windshields
31. Put purse on passenger seat, within easy reach
32. Put car into gear
33. Wind down driver's window
34. Put left arm out window and shake to get all 27 bracelets positioned correctly on   arm
35. Adjust skirt
36. Check rear view mirror
37. Drive away

God-Almighty-Damn!!! Every man who has ever watched a woman get into a car and prepare to operate it has seen this scenario time and again. And, Guys, if you can watch it and get through it without physically attacking the woman in question, you don't need to live with a cat or read any more of this book. You are ready - more than ready - to share your home and your life with a woman.

25. Cats
Traveling

Cats hate to travel. They hate cars, they hate planes, they hate any environment in which they are not in complete control. When first coerced into a car, the cat will give you its most piteous yowl: *"Oh, shit, not the car again, Human, **please** don't make me stay in here, I really, really hate it here, please let me out, please, I promise I'll never crap in your philodendron again, Human, please, not the car, **noooooo**!!!"* Then, when she sees she won't be getting out anytime soon *(and as long as she's not in the cat carrier, which she knows is preparatory to going to the vet),* she'll slink away under the seat and hunker down, and every once in awhile you'll hear her, *"I really hate it under here, Human, because I'm not in control in the car and you'd better let me out of here damn soon or every one of your cashmere sweaters is fucking **toast!**"* yowl.

And speaking of cat carriers, have you ever tried to get a cat into one? Cats must be genetically programmed to recognize and fear cat carriers. As soon as they see one, they instinctively know what it's for, and they shoot out the cat door, or race for the deepest, darkest corner under the bed. And not even catnip will bring them back. So, Guys, it's best to use sneakiness and guile to get the cat into the carrier.

First of all, don't even think about the carrier or destination for at least an hour before you want to leave. Cats seem to have an extra sensory gene that lets them know when you are even slightly considering just possibly taking them somewhere in the cat carrier. Just let the mere *thought* of a cat carrier cross your mind and the cat's ears immediately perk up, his eyes widen in fear and acknowledgment of what might come, and he's off in a record-breaking hundred-yard-dash for the nearest rooftop or deepest, darkest corner of the attic. And he won't come down/out until well after midnight, when he judges it's safe to check out the food bowl again.

So, mind focused on your date tomorrow night, and before you put on your coat or pick up the car keys or get the cat carrier from its closet storage place, look at your cat and say to it, in a completely normal tone of voice, "You know, Samson, you haven't had a cat treat for awhile. How about some Little Friskies snacks? Hah? Whaddaya say, Big Guy?" Then go to the cat treat cupboard and take out the cat treats. The cat will know what you're doing, and will follow you all the way, mewling expectantly and piteously.

"Little Friskies cat treats? Hah, Human? I love those, especially the fish-flavored ones. Can I have one of those today, hah? Please, Human? Ooooo, thanks, yummy, yummy, so good. Another? Please? Why are you picking me up, Human, you can give me the cat treat here on the floor, I don't mind, really. Wait a minute, where are we going? I can smell the treat in your hand, can I have it, please? Why are we going toward the closet? What's in.......Aaaaaaaaarrrrggghhh, nooooo, not the Cat Carrier, no please, no, why now, I was having such a good time, where are we going, not the vet, surely?"

As you open the closet door and remove the cat carrier, the cat's yowls increase in piteousness. But then, when you open the cat carrier's door and try to put the cat inside, the cat turns from docile, lazy, well-groomed house cat into The Feline Dynamo. She sees that black hole and grabs the sides of the cat carrier door opening with all four paws and refuses to be shoved inside. You can push and shove and curse, but the cat will not be moved. The only way to get him into the carrier, Guys, is to revert to kitten treatment - yep, pick the cat up by the scruff of its neck and lower him gently into the carrier. He'll go, because he has no choice when picked up like that, but he won't like it. In fact, if you want him to speak to you again anytime soon, you'll have a nice fat mouse in the carrier for him to play with and while away the time until you're ready to set him free once again. Cats dearly hate cat carriers.

But even more, they hate leashes. Leashes are for dogs, and cats know this. The reason cats hate leashes is they hate being treated like a dog. Never attempt to take your cat for a walk like a dog. You can carry a cat in your arms, but you can not get her to walk at the end of a leash. Cats are free spirits and rebel furiously at being confined or restrained in any way. The cat's pathetic yowls at such treatment are, first, designed to melt the heart of even the harshest Human and, second, will then turn into such outraged screams of mortification that you will immediately and without further thought release the cat from its bondage, no questions asked. A cat is a tough partner, and will brook no restrictions on its movements. Now come on, Guys, doesn't all this remind you of someone you know?

26. Women Traveling

Women, on the other hand love to travel to exotic destinations. Actually, I should say, they love *arriving* at exotic destinations. It's the in-between times they dislike, the moving from one place to another. Because they are not in control of their environment. And the type of traveling they hate the most, in order, is:

(1) By car, when they are expected to drive or read a map. For some reason, the map-reading gene of most women seems to have atrophied to the point of non-existence. So, guys, never ask a woman to read a map. She just can't do it. It's not her fault, it's just the way things are. She is just not genetically programmed to read a map. Women excel, however, at stopping. Stopping to shop, to use the restroom, to buy a soda, to get out of the hated car and stretch for awhile. Sort of like the cat, actually.

As a matter of fact, women really only put up with automobile trips when they can act as the backseat driver. They love this role, because it allows them to cover up their innate fear of traveling in the car. See, Guys, just like the cat, a woman truly hates and despises vehicular travel, and for essentially the same reason as the cat - she loses control of her environment, which is the be-all and end-all for every woman ever born. Control over her life, home (cave), family, kitchen, clothes, shoes, and, with certain reservations and a lot of trepidation, the family car.

Women seem to be genetically programmed to respond negatively to all forms of motion and movement not initiated by themselves. As long as they start the movement, they remain in control of their means of transportation, and thus of their life and their fate. But let someone else get behind the wheel of the family station wagon, and the woman reverts immediately to Fear-Filled Cavewoman, ever afraid of the hostile environment just the other side of her property line. An area over which she has no control. Thus emergeth the screeching harpy, screaming directions and instructions and unwanted advice to the long-suffering husband/boyfriend/whatever. It's just her fear driving her to it, Guys, so suck it up and ignore any and all nonsensical ramblings from the actual or metaphorical rear seat. She just can't help it.

*(Ed Note: The Fear of Automobile Analogy breaks down when the woman gets to travel in a luxury car, like a Rolls Royce or Bentley or Testarossa [with an automatic transmission, of course, since women can't shift and use the clutch at the same time]. Luxurious surroundings and expensive things **always** bury deeply any fears the woman may have regarding uncontrolled motion, since Money Talks. The woman can now feel superior to every other human being on the planet and thus her mundane fears are pushed so far into the background that she refuses to give them any credence. You didn't think she latched onto you for your looks, Bud, now did you?)*

(2) By plane. Man, if you think a woman has a hard time traveling by car, wait till you see her board an airplane. Her Fear Compensation Factor immediately shifts into high gear, taking the guise of: tear-filled appeals for an upgrade to business or first class; blocking the aisle for as long as possible while stuffing her carry-on bags into the overhead bin, thus hopefully delaying the flight for just a little bit longer; buying all of the items in the duty-free catalogue; calling all of her friends on the in-flight telephone attached to the seat-back in front of her; bugging the stewardess

(apologies to the flight attendants reading this book, but when I started flying the female flight attendants were called stewardesses, and that's what I'm calling them until I die) for magazines, drinks, extra rolls and paper towels. *(Ed Note: The stewardesses, being mostly women themselves, understand the reason behind Everywoman's badgering, and thus are ever-patient with their traveling sisters, giving them whatever they ask for without even a minor quiver).*

(3) By train. Not usually so bad, since the train is on solid ground (well, railroad tracks) and is sort of like a really big car - or mobile home - so the woman can walk around and feel somewhat safe and in general control of her environment. Better than an automobile, anyway.

(4) By escalator. Ever watch a woman as she tries her fearful best to take that first step onto a moving escalator? You'd think she was putting her leg into a meat grinding machine. As the line to use the escalator grows longer and longer behind her, she tentatively eases one foot forward, slowly, slowly, while trying to hold onto the moving rail and her purse and packages, and then letting the rail slip through her fingers and stepping back quickly, shoving the people in line behind her even farther back, and then, quickly, lest she lose her nerve, stepping onto that first - or second - or third - moving step and being jerked backwards, but grasping

the moving handrail in a death grip and **she's on!** Successful completion of The Escalator Line Dance. Made it. Getting off, of course, is another adventure entirely, but she's safe for the moment so we'll leave her on the escalator and move on.

Of course, the Traveling Woman is also incapable of leaving home, even for an afternoon's outing, without all of the "necessities" of her life: an entire department store cosmetics counter of toiletries; fourteen complete changes of clothing (from underwear to raincoats); an automotive store's complete stock of spare parts for the car; and a purse-full of enough food and drink to keep a family of four alive for a month. Just in case, you understand. Gotta control her environment to the nth degree.

Leaving the cave is just as scary a proposition for a woman today as it was for her long-ago cave-dwelling ancestress. Large animals with fangs and claws might be lurking outside, nasty two-legged predators might be nearby and - Holy Forgotten Box of Kleenex, Batman - there might even be several miles between shoe stores! Not a chance in hell that any woman ever born will ever leave her home without a duplicate of every piece of clothing and every item of furniture and every tube and vial of cosmetics she owns. Reconcile yourselves, men, women take their environment with them.

27. Cats
Primary Weapons

Cats have their own ways of getting even with us for real or imagined offenses against their dignity, sense of control over their environment *(like forcing them to take a ride in the car)* or forgetting to feed them on time. First of all, they can give us a new yowl, one we haven't heard before, one which clearly (to the cat, anyway) says, *"Hey, Human, get with the program and give me what I want. I can keep this yowling up all day and night, and you can forget about sleeping for the next few days."*

Or, the cat can casually stroll over to our $20,000 combination stereo/video/personal computer setup and wet it down with spray or cat urine. That'll teach you, Human!

Or, the cat can wait until we've gone to work for the day and then proceed to sharpen its claws on every single fabric in the house: drapes, sofa covers, bedspreads, suits, sweaters, Turkish carpets, bath towels and lampshades. Then, not completely satisfied with this partial destruction of our habitat, they go on to shred videotapes, use our Bally loafers as a toilet, and knock over the trash can and rummage through whatever they can find strewn across the floor.

As a last gasp, they use their cat door to go outside and capture a couple of birds, which they then bring into the house and let free to fly around and knock down various lamps and items of artwork they can't reach and to crap all over our favorite recliner. If they could, they'd probably also turn on the gas and blow up the whole damn house. *"Okay, Human, NOW will you treat me right?"*

Amazingly to us humans, the cat's malice apparently knows no bounds, and the cat actually seems to glory in the destruction it causes. The pure cat joy the cat feels in using its teeth and claws is such that it needs no real excuse to employ its offensive and defensive mechanisms. It just uses them for sheer pleasure. Ripping up our camel-hair coat is just gravy. It's the act itself that counts. And spraying our new stereo?! Wow, power!

"I am Cat, hear me yowl! Watch me shred and spray! I am the all-powerful, the all-knowing, the amazinglyweaponed Cat! Fail to give me gourmet cat food or scratch my chin or stroke me just right, Human, and suffer the consequences. These claws aren't just for catching mice and stuff. They'll make short shrift of your new alpaca sweater, just like its cashmere predecessor. And these teeth can bite an unsuspecting mouse cleanly in half. So be careful, Human. I am faster and stronger and smarter than you are. Even if I can't work the can opener to get at the gourmet cat food!"

28. Women

Primary Weapons

A woman's penultimate weapon, of course, is tears. Let her start to scrunch up her face and begin to leak salt water out of her eyes and most men are reduced to helplessness. Are we guys genetically programmed to react this way to such an obvious manipulation of our emotions?

On the other hand, a woman's argument, naturally, incorporates all sorts of confusing logic and non sequiturs and accusations which are not germane to the topic being argued about. She will get nasty and sarcastic *(in fact, catty)*. She will belittle our earning potential, sneer at our hairstyle and impugn our sexuality and lovemaking techniques. No blow is too low for an arguing woman. She will bare her (metaphorical) claws and fangs, and go directly for our balls. Winning the argument is, to a woman, critical and mandatory.

Failure to win an argument means the woman no longer has control over her environment and her life and her mate. A situation which cannot be tolerated. She will use any and every weapon in her arsenal to defeat us, and we, as men, must never forget it.

When backed into a (metaphorical) corner, and she is in danger of losing the argument, a woman will instantly call into action her next-to-last weapon: tears. Any man worth his salt, and older than the age of seven, has, however, learned to recognize this ploy and will no longer fall for it. When the tears start, Men, stand quietly and let your woman sob and leak tears and generally work herself into a pretty sad state, mascara running freely down her cheeks, hair in disarray, stockings torn, gasping and, *(she hopes we think so)*, completely out of control. Eventually, of course, she will peek out between her fingers and see that this defense just doesn't work anymore. Watch her carefully and, with practice, you will be able to determine when your woman reaches this point and you will be able to prepare yourself for Phase Two and for the introduction of the woman's Big Gun, her Ultimate Weapon. And we all know what that is, don't we, Guys?

A woman's primary, and final, weapon, naturally, is the withholding of physical pleasures from her man. Since sex is all we really want anyway, this weapon can have a serious effect on most men. Our options in the face of such a weapon are limited, but no less powerful for that. We can go off to our den and turn on a football game and open a beer and sulk for several hours; which, of course, does us no good at all and plays right into the woman's game plan of wearing us down until we do what she want us to do.

Some women devise other means of getting to us when they've lost an argument or we otherwise won't do what they want, like cutting the sleeves off our suit coats or not speaking to us *(which, they never seem to realize, is actually a blessing in disguise - ah, the silence is deafening!).*

Or, we can hie ourselves off to our favorite neighborhood bar, where we know we can find our friendly neighborhood party girl, who will take us home with her and screw our brains out and thus we can get revenge over the little woman, who won't be enjoying our physical pleasuring.

Or we can come all over Tarzan and pick up the offending woman and run up the staircase and throw her on the bed and ravish her until she screams for mercy - or more ravishing, whichever comes first.

Or, we can shove a grapefruit in her face..

19. Cats

Defending Yourself Against Them

Taking it as a given that you can't *(or don't want to)* strangle your cat for her seeming transgressions against you *(which, after all, are merely manifestations of her essential catness),* there are very few methods of retaliation against an offending cat.

1. You can take the cat to the vet for shots, a checkup, a long wait in the waiting room with a bunch of impatient dogs, a little "snip and tuck," etc. Cats, like most other animals, hate the veterinarian and will do whatever it takes to avoid a trip to same. First of all, of course, you have to catch the cat. The cat is smart, often smarter than you, and can tell just by the tone in your voice that a trip to the vet is imminent. You may think your call of "Here, kitty, kitty, come on, kitty, come and get your nice kitty treat," will lure the cat to you with no fuss or bother, and you can then pop her

into the cat carrier *(which you **must** keep hidden until time for occupancy, lest the cat suspect what is about to happen; see Chapter 25).*

Beware the sin of pride, my son. The cat knows that wheedling tone of voice and will take to the roof of the house until said tone is no more. It is much better not to say or do anything out of the ordinary. Since you will have to use the cat carrier on several occasions during the year, it is best to reiterate the tactics needed to get the cat into it. First, leave the cat carrier in the closet. Wait until dinnertime and call the cat in your normal voice, while holding a can of its favorite wet cat food. When the cat hears the first whirr of the automatic can opener, she will dash from her hiding place and race to your side. You can then pick her up casually, walk to the closet, lift out the cat carrier, open its door and put the cat into it before it knows what's happened.

Of course, you had best then step back smartly and close the carrier door quickly, lest the cat gouge several furrows into your forearm for being tricked so heinously. She won't trust you for awhile, and will forever after even be a touch wary of dinnertime. So much the better for your peace of mind. Keeping the cat guessing and off-balance makes for a much better relationship between Man and Cat.

2. Barring strangulation, you can heave the cat over into the neighbor's yard, wherein lurks the neighbor's killer German Shepherd. The cat may not like you for awhile, but a nice can of fresh wet cat food should restore normalcy. Besides, cats don't get nearly enough exercise and this will be good for her.

30. Women

Defending Yourself Against

Okay, Men, pay attention here. You won't see this type of advice in Cosmo or Playboy. Keep in mind that the woman always has the last word in any argument. Anything you may say after that is actually the beginning of another argument. Of course, Men, you'll have to practice determining which word ends the present argument and where the next argument begins, but be assured you will have plenty of practice.

The easiest way to defend yourself against your woman is to disarm her, steer her attention away from the argument and onto another subject. Chocolates are always a good disarmament tool. While she's yakking and badgering away at you, grab a large box of chocolates from the desktop and open it and go through the process of selecting your favorite. Be sure she can see into the box, and be sure the box contains her favorite chocolates. She'll usually frown and creep closer to the chocolates to see what remains in the box. When she snatches a cream-filled chocolate bon-bon, you've won. *(Predictable as a curious cat, hah?)*

If you've screwed up and forgotten to stock the house with chocolates, you can use appropriate substitutes: jewelry works well, as do flowers. Anything to disarm the little woman and divert her attention away from your real or imagined sin and onto something else. "Gee, dear, I was saving this for your birthday, but I guess now is as good a time as any to give you this diamond pendant. I hope you like it." Nice going, Sport, she's effectively diverted. There may still be a little residual animosity, but generally you've won again.

Of course, you can also do to a woman what she does to us: Agree with her. Agree to do whatever she wants you to do, then go ahead and do what you wanted to in the first place. This response drives women absolutely bonkers, because they don't think we know this trick of theirs. They hate having their tricks turned against them, but they are powerless to respond because they know that your response is what they would do - have done - in your place. But, hey, all's fair in love and relationships.

Since women must feel in control of relationships, their environment and their man, let her win the argument and, if it comes to it, let her break up with you. Pretend to a humility you don't feel and you'll get off easy. But if you win the argument *(telling a woman you don't agree with her is the same, to her, as telling her you don't love her)*, or you do the breaking up, it drives a woman crazy and she will keep picking away at you until she believes she's won or broken up. Let them have their perceived triumphs, Guys. It's worth it. They think they have upper hand and are in control, and this keeps them complacent and in their place. We really get the best of both worlds.

31. Cats
Getting on Our Case

Sometimes the cat just will not leave us alone. She demands attention, and usually at the most inopportune time: while we're trying to complete an important report for work; adjusting the timing on the car; removing the panties from a great weekend date. At such times, you must be patient and tactful with the cat. Getting angry with her won't help and will just serve to make the cat increase its efforts to get your attention. As in the case of women, try a diversion. Catnip, chocolates, a new toy. *(Ed. Note: Jewelry and flowers don't usually work with cats.)*

Usually, the cat will leave us to our own devices, as she's content to go her own way and to live her own life. But every now and then, she wants what she wants when she wants it, which is *"**NOW, Human!** Pay attention to me. I want my chin chucked **NOW**!"*

The cat will head-butt you on your beer-holding arm while you're trying to watch the football game, getting more and more insistent for attention. She will weave in and out of our legs while we're trying to put on our pants, thus causing us at least annoyance, and at most a stumbling fall against the side of the dresser and a nice gash in the head.

Ignore the cat at your peril. You'll find opposite-colored hair on your clothes and chairs and sofas. Your remaining cashmere sweater will end up with tiny kneaded cashmere balls all over it and will be useful only for collection by Goodwill. You'll revel in being able to sleep in one Saturday morning, only to wake up to find The Cat batting at your nose with its cute little paws, sometimes even with its claws retracted. Lucky you. And when the cat spies one eye opening even a slit, she'll start pouncing up and down on you and jumping on your chest and generally making a pest of herself until you acknowledge her existence and drag your poor hungover self out of bed and give the cat some gourmet cat food. Oh Rapturous/Frabjous Day!

32. Women

Getting on Our Case

Every woman should see the movie *Jackie Brown* to drive this point home to them. Bridget Fonda berates Robert DeNiro for bungling an otherwise easy minor criminal act. He advises her to be quiet. She starts in on him again. He tells her to shut up. Nope, she comes back at him yet again! He wheels on her and says, in that flinty, no-nonsense voice, "Not another SOUND!" then turns to walk away. Three quiet seconds go by and she, female that she is, and not taking him seriously, and, in fact, genetically unable to keep quiet, makes that sound: "You....." And he whirls around once more and blows her away with his .45 automatic.

Women just never learn. They can push us and push us and push us - but only so far. And they seem genetically incapable of recognizing when they reach that "so far" point. So they push us again - and are amazed when they immediately suffer the consequences of their continued bugging. Be warned, Women of the World - you had better learn where that "No Push" zone starts. Go watch *Jackie Brown* again. Take notes. Learn from your experiences. And, by the way -- give us sex, which is all we really want anyway!

In short, Guys, women just do not listen! We can tell them and tell them and warn them and plead with them, and they'll still do whatever they want to do. Exactly like that damn cat! They seem to be genetically incapable of listening to and hearing and actually digesting and, even more, paying attention to anything and everything a man says. Apparently, women have either an extra *"I Don't Hear You"* gene, or they lack a *"I Hear You Clearly and I Understand Exactly What You Want"* gene.

Any man who has ever attempted to convince a woman of anything, using his best and most persuasive and most rational arguments and hard-learned Aristotelian Logic can be called into court and sworn in to testify that a woman never listens to or hears anything a man has to say. A woman only hears the little voice inside her own head that tells her to go ahead and do exactly what she wants to do, and never mind that strange buzzing sound in her ears, as it's only a man making no sense whatsoever - at least, to her. Pay attention, Guys, this is important stuff. You will be tested on it later - no, Bozo, not in this book - in real life by your female roommate, girlfriend, wife, whatever.

The day will come when you'll bring to bear all of your best and most reasonable reasons and arguments as to why the living together situation is perfectly adequate for you both, and you see no need reason to change anything - nay, to spoil anything - by getting married. I mean, look what marriage did to your best friends: that beautiful church wedding, the perfect couple, two beautiful children, nice house, car, great jobs - and divorced after just five short years of marital bliss.

Neither you nor your girlfriend need the marriage hassle. You are Clarence Darrow and Daniel Webster rolled into one. The schools would have been teaching evolution years ago, and the devil would have rolled over with his paws in the air and given up in the face of your beautifully reasoned arguments. Plato and Aristotle would have had you teaching their classes. No more perfectly-reasoned arguments have existed since classical Greece. But does your woman understand? Does she hear you? Is she even listening to your dulcet tones, dripping with reason and persuasion? Not a chance in hell, Bud. You just wasted three good hours, when you could have been golfing or watching football. She hasn't really heard a word you've said. Her mind was made up before you even started to speak. You lost before you began.

Did you notice that all during your closing argument to the jury of one that she was looking at you as if she really cared what you had to say? Her head nodded regularly, up and down, up and down, like that little dog in the rear window of your car. She smiled constantly at you and said, "Uh huh," and "Okay," and "Sure thing," at appropriate intervals. And then, when you finally ran out of steam and words, she looked at you and said, "We're getting married next month or I'm out of here - but not before I cut all the sleeves off your suit coats."

Did not hear a single word you said! Her *"I Don't Hear You"* gene kicked in as soon as the words, "Marriage will just spoil our great relationship" spilled forth from your mouth. After that, you were just creating a slight breeze as you flapped your lips. Wake Up, Bud - SHE CAN'T HEAR YOU! A woman is genetically incapable of hearing anything she doesn't want to hear. Learn this fact, live with it, deal with it. Find ways around it. But never, never attempt to meet it head on. You can not win. She's got you licked before you even start.

Learn evasive tactics. Discuss the importance of her job. Compliment her on her new perfume. Work the discussion around to how you think you might be able to afford that new car she's been hinting about. Or start in on this year's vacation to Hawaii or Aruba or Paris. Deflect, circumvent, divert. Yes, of course it's only a temporary diversion, but that's all we men can really hope for at best. We know, in our heart of hearts, we'll eventually give in. We always do. But it should be on our terms, not hers. Hang tough, Guys. The longer you put off marriage and commitment, the longer the sex stays great. Which is all we really want anyway.

33. Training A Cat
Good Luck

Weeeeelllll, maybe, Guys, but you better have infinite patience and you better also find a cat that, despite its own peculiar ideas about Cat-dom, feels like doing what you want it to do. I know, I know, there are documented cases of men training a cat to use the toilet in the bathroom. Or of men training cats to raise an alarm when it smells smoke. Or of men (and I am one!) training a cat to sit and beg when it wants food. Or of men training cats to bring them a beer while they're watching the football game on TV. *(Okay, I made that last one up, but a really big cat could probably do it, right?).*

In short, it is marginally possible to train a cat to do certain things and carry out certain tasks, but - and this is the kicker - only if the cat really wants to. See, the cat only lets us *think* it has been trained. It is really doing just what it wants to do, and always for reasons of its own. These reasons usually involve food or extended freedom to roam around outside the confines of the house.

Of course, training a cat takes infinite patience and good humor and sturdy leather clothing, as the cat, always wanting to control its environment, will, at first, not take kindly to being manipulated and will ignore all attempts to get it to do what you want. *(Are you sure this doesn't sound familiar, Guys?)*. The Cat will walk disdainfully away, its tail high in the air, its little rump swaying scornfully from side to side, uttering its "Don't even *think* about trying to train me, Human; not a chance in hell!" yowl echoing behind it.

Subsequent attempts at training will be met with a supercilious silence and a superior air of nonchalance. The cat seems to be saying, "Well, Human, your pathetic attempts at training are laughable in the extreme, but I *might* be amenable to thinking about doing what you want if offered the right incentive." Once you reach this point, Men, after months of rejection and spurned dignity, you might want to keep one word foremost in your mind: Incentives. What *can* you offer the cat to do what you want? Well, of course, the most obvious is food. Catnip-laced tuna fish. Real mouse livers. Chopped-up swordfish. Even a live bird, if you're really serious about all this. Flowers and jewelry work well with a woman, but the cat needs something a touch more substantial.

So, now you're on your way, Guys. Keep at it, slowly, patiently, ploddingly, and, if the cat feels like it, it will eventually come around. With a disdainful yawn and a twitch of its tail, the cat will think, *"Well, okay Human, what the hell, you've worked hard enough and I guess I've gotten as many extras out of you as I can expect, so why not? Besides, using the human toilet is kind of cool. None of my cat friends can do that. And, if it will increase the size of the offering, I guess I can sit and beg for the right kind and amount of food. So, we'll compromise: I'll do what you want me to and you'll give me everything I want in order for me to do what you want. Get it? That's a cat's idea of compromise."* Congratulations, Men, you now have a trained cat.

34. Training A Woman
You Must be Joking!

Get serious, Guys. You don't really think a woman can be trained like a pet, do you? Those days went out with women's suffrage and women managers and PMS recognition and women's kickboxing tournaments. The other half of the human race has made its presence known, has booted Pandora out of her box and is on a roll. "I am woman, hear me roar!" Those roars are getting louder and louder, threatening to drown out traditional male roles and to take over the male-dominant (and dominated) societies which have existed for a couple of thousand years. Women are here to stay and they will no longer accept the age-old roles of housemaker and baby-factory.

Of course, insidious beasts that we are, we men know there are some things we can do to get a woman to do our bidding. Such things always, of course, involve unusually large expenditures of cash. The bigger the thing you want them to do, the more money you have to spend. Forget the old "Bringing Her Breakfast in Bed," or "Taking Out The Trash" (which she thinks is our duty anyway), or "Surprising Her With Flowers When It's Not Her Birthday." These ploys may have worked for your grandfather, but you don't have time for ploying around. Nope, gotta go right for the jugular. Cash is a touch vulgar, but a really nice tennis bracelet or a new Mercedes XL4000 will definitely put you on the right track to success.

Naturally, Men, you must realize that, unlike the cat, a woman will probably not stay trained. Women are notoriously fickle and will revert to type the instant they think they are not in control of the situation and are being cleverly manipulated by us. Gotta be really careful, Guys. Subtlety, Gents, that's the key. Keep them off balance just enough, with small, but thoughtful, gifts and presents, and once in awhile a really nice big extravagant, expensive gift, and you can usually keep them just quiescent enough to thankfully bring you that beer while you're watching the game, or to make your favorite meal on a weekday, or to let you have a monthly poker game with your buddies, or, of course, to give you more frequent and better and more experimental sex. Which is all we really want anyway.

However - and this is a BIG HOWEVER, Guys, there are a few things you can and should try to make clear to your woman. Training is pretty much out of the question, but, with patience and forbearance, you can subtly communicate your desires, wishes and, dare we say it, guidelines, for entering into a healthy relationship with your woman. I wouldn't go so far as to call these guidelines rules *(although, if we're honest with ourselves, we'd sure like to make them such),* but if you can let your female partner know how you feel about these things that are of importance to you, you've gone a long way to establishing the type of relationship you want and expect, i.e., one where you - the Herd Bull - are in charge. Keep in mind the following, and do your level best to let her know - nicely, my boy, nicely - how you expect things to be in your mutual home.

Things You Should Tell Your Female Partner:

Learn to work the toilet seat. You're a big girl. If it's up, put it down. We need it up, you need it down. You don't hear us complaining about you leaving it down.

Whenever possible, please say whatever you have to say during commercials.

A headache that lasts for 17 months is a problem. See a doctor.

Sunday = sports. It's like the full moon or the changing of the tides. Let it be.

Shopping is NOT a sport. And no, we are never going to think of it that way.

Crying is blackmail *(see Chapter 30)*.

Ask for what you want. Let us be clear on this one: Subtle hints do not work! Strong hints do not work! Obvious hints do not work! Just say it!

Yes and No are perfectly acceptable answers to almost every question.

Come to us with a problem only if you want help solving it. That's what we do. Sympathy is what your girlfriends are for.

Anything we said six months ago is inadmissible in an argument. In fact, all comments become null and void after seven days.

If something we said can be interpreted two ways, and one of the ways makes you sad or angry, we meant the other one.

You can either ask us to do something or tell us how you want it done. Not both. If you already know best how to do it, just do it yourself.

Christopher Columbus did not need directions and neither do we.

ALL men see in only 16 colors, like Windows default settings. Peach, for example, is a fruit, not a color. Pumpkin is also a fruit. We have no idea what mauve is.

If it itches, it will be scratched. We do that.

If we ask what is wrong and you say "nothing," we will act like nothing's wrong. We know you are lying, but it's not worth the hassle.

If you ask a question you don't want an answer to, expect an answer you don't want to hear.

When we have to go somewhere, absolutely anything you wear is fine. Really.

Don't ask us what we're thinking - unless you are prepared to discuss such topics as baseball, sports, Charlize Theron, or fast cars.

You have enough clothes.

You have too many shoes.

Finally, Men, when you have exhausted yourself setting forth your guidelines, you may thank her for listening to you. Of course, you'll have to sleep on the couch for a few nights, but, you know, women don't realize that men really don't mind that, it's like going camping.

Okay, Gents, that's about the furthest you can expect to go in the Training Your Woman department. If you can get your partner to agree to ANY ONE of these hopes and expectations, you can then write your own book on how to live with a woman; you've obviously far surpassed my humble efforts.

Conclusion

So, Guys, there you have it. It should be obvious by now, even to the thickest man, that cats and women may belong to different races, but that, in fact, they are the same species. Men, you can practice living with a cat before you take the plunge and try living with a woman. You can do it. Your life with a cat will prepare you for the more challenging, but basically the same, type of life with a woman.

Still not sure? C'mon, Men, the parallels are everywhere. When one woman is nasty and mean and condescending to another woman, when she tears her down and rips her up, why do we call the first woman "catty?" (And by the way, Guys, notice the use of the words *rip* and *tear*. Words usually used to describe something done with claws.). Why do so many women prefer to keep a cat as a pet rather than a dog? Does the phrase *same species* ring a bell?

And if you ever have the chance to witness two women in a physical confrontation, a "girl fight tonight," watch how they fight. They claw at each other's hair. They bite. They scratch. They gouge. Cats, Guys, they're cats! Still not convinced? It wasn't so long ago that a beautiful woman was referred to as "the cat's meow." And mens' nicknames for women? Pussycat? Kitten? And, if one wishes to be vulgar this late in the book (which your author never is!), one could point out the puerile slang name for a woman's private area - but one won't. You already know it.

Even when women relax, they only relax completely with someone they trust. Or with someone over whom they hold absolute power. The woman lies spread-limbed on the Barcalounger, completely at ease with her environment. In control. Relaxed, yet watchful. Always checking the house and the immediate vicinity, always looking for the attack. They continue to test their mate, to ensure fidelity and obedience and a six-figure annual income.

Guys, you should now have a good idea of how to handle your recalcitrant cat. Take all of the information in this book and put it to good use. Get yourself a kitten and raise it and train it as you know now you are capable of doing. Get comfortable with the cat. Develop a relationship, with yourself in the driver's seat, naturally.

And when you're ready, when you know all the ins and outs of dealing with your cat, go out and get yourself a woman and ask her to live with you. Confidence and belief in your abilities to deal with her should result in the most satisfying relationship of your life. You'll have everything you always dreamed of, and you will have had the upper hand in getting it. And you'll get lots and lots of great sex. Which is all we really want anyway.

You are now ready! Good luck, Men. Rowwwwr.

About The Author

Gary Lukatch was born in St. Louis, Missouri, before the term "Baby Boomer" was coined. He has lived in eight American states and two foreign countries - so far!. Upon graduating from the University of Missouri with a degree in Political Science, he served in the United States Army and was awarded the Good Conduct Medal. He then spent 29 years in the financial industry in California, New Mexico, Texas and Nevada. In 1999 he finally had enough. He quit his job, sold his house, sold his car, sold his furniture, threw his briefcase into the San Francisco Bay, got a tattoo, took a course in Teaching English as a Foreign Language and moved to Central Europe. He now teaches Business English to the English-starved business people of Budapest, Hungary.

He is the author of three other published works: *To Úr With Love,* a romp through his second life (i.e., his move to and early days in Budapest); *Bankers' Hours,* a romp through his first life in the financial business in southern California; and *Summers' Time,* a romp among the women of Central and Eastern Europe. The first two are available on *authorhouse.com* and *amazon.com*; the third is available from the author. He has also written many C&W song lyrics, sadly all unpublished and unsung, including such should-be classics as: *If I'd Have Met You Sooner I'd Be Through With You By Now*; *I Can't Get Over You 'Till You Get Out From Under Him*; *If You Can't Live Without Me, How Come You Aren't Dead*; *She's Got A World Class Body And The Face To Guard It With*; and his own personal favorite, *The Ballad of Onan.*

He has been inside an Egyptian pyramid in Giza, visited a Turkish Bath in Istanbul, backed up quickly from the snake charmers in Marrakech, crewed an America's Cup racing yacht and climbed the Leaning Tower of Pisa. He has visited the still-dead-but-looking-really-good V.I. Lenin in Moscow's Red Square, flashed Beverly Hills, been a weight-lifting champion, floated in the Dead Sea, and eaten "haggis reeking, wi' bashed neeps" in Edinburgh, Scotland.

He has his name on an Olympic brick in Atlanta, Georgia, and his picture in the Tropical Isle Bar in New Orleans, Louisiana (at last sighting). He has scuba-dived the Cozumel reefs and skied Mt. Etna. He has even taught English in Oxford, England. He once owned a goat, but he NEVER owned a Leisure Suit. He has lived with seven different cats and three very different women. These days he can often be found at The Caledonia Pub in Budapest, Hungary, quaffing Scottish beer and singing karaoke.

And for those of you who are REALLY interested in him, he can be contacted at:

Teachrman@yahoo.com.